AIR FRYER TOASTER OVEN COOKBOOK

A Comprehensive Guide to Effortless and Tasty Recipes. Transform Your Meals with Quick, Easy, and Healthy Frying, Baking, Toasting, and Roasting Tips.

URSULA F. GRAY

Copyright © 2024 By URSULA F. GRAY. All rights reserved worldwide.

No part of this book may be reproduced or transmitted in any form or by any means, electronic or mechanical, including photocopying, recording, or by any information storage and retrieval system, without written permission from the publisher, except for the inclusion of brief quotations in a review.

Warning-Disclaimer:

The purpose of this book is to educate and entertain. The author or publisher does not guarantee that anyone following the techniques, suggestions, tips, ideas, or strategies will become successful. The author and publisher shall have neither liability nor responsibility to anyone with respect to any loss or damage caused, or alleged to be caused, directly or indirectly, by the information contained in this book.

This copyright notice and disclaimer apply to the entirety of the book and its contents, whether in print or electronic form, and extend to all future editions or revisions of the book. Unauthorized use or reproduction of this book or its contents is strictly prohibited and may result in legal action.

TABLE OF CONTENTS

INTRODUCTION 5
    BENEFITS 7
    OVERVIEW 9

CHAPTER 1: APPETIZERS & SNACKS 11
    Crispy Air Fryer Chickpeas 11
    Veggie Fritters with Yogurt Dip 11
    Coconut Shrimp with Sweet Chili Sauce 12
    Air Fryer Blooming Onion 12
    Spicy Buffalo Cauliflower Bites 13
    Loaded Air Fryer Nachos 13
    Crispy Avocado Fries 14
    Bacon Wrapped Tater Tots 15
    Pesto Stuffed Mushrooms 15
    Churro Bites 16

CHAPTER 2: BREAKFAST & BRUNCH 17
    Air Fryer Bacon & Egg Cups 17
    Overnight Cinnamon Rolls 17
    Hash Brown Breakfast Casserole 17
    Frittata Muffins with Spinach & Feta 18
    Air Fryer Doughnuts 18
    Breakfast Sausage Patties 19
    French Toast Sticks 19
    Mini Quiches 19
    Home Fries 20
    Air Fryer Breakfast Burritos 20

CHAPTER 3: VEGETARIAN MAINS 22
    Black Bean & Quinoa Burgers 22
    Cauliflower Buffalo Bites 22
    Crispy Air Fryer Falafel 23
    Baked Stuffed Tomatoes 23
    Vegetable Pakoras 24
    Mediterranean Stuffed Peppers 24
    Butternut Squash & Kale Quesadillas 25
    Lentil Sloppy Joes 25
    Baked Veggie Egg Rolls 26
    BBQ Jackfruit Sandwiches 26

CHAPTER 4: MEAT & POULTRY 28
    Perfect Air Fryer Steak 28
    Crispy Parmesan Chicken Tenders 28
    Cajun Spiced Pork Chops 29

Honey Garlic Drumsticks 29
Meatballs with Marinara Sauce 30
Philly Cheesesteak Stuffed Peppers 30
Air Fryer Turkey Burgers 31
Coconut Lime Chicken Skewers 31
Glazed Air Fryer Ham 32
Greek Beef Kabobs 32

CHAPTER 5: SEAFOOD 34

Coconut Shrimp with Pineapple Salsa 34
Lemon Dill Salmon Patties 34
Crispy Fried Fish Sandwiches 35
Cajun Air Fryer Shrimp 35
Pesto Crusted Salmon Fillets 36
Tuna Poke Bowl 36
Asian Glazed Cod 37
Shrimp Fajitas 37
Crab Cake Sliders 38
Crispy Calamari 38

CHAPTER 6: PASTA, PIZZA & BREADS 39

Personal Deep Dish Pizzas 39
Garlic Knots 39
Baked Pasta Bites 40
Air Fryer Bagels 40
Calzones 41
Chili Cheese Stuffed Pretzels 41
Air Fryer Empanadas 42
Toasted Ravioli Bites 42
Cheesy Garlic Breadsticks 43
Stromboli 43

CHAPTER 7: VEGETABLES & SIDES 44

Crispy Air Fryer Brussel Sprouts 44
Parmesan Roasted Asparagus 44
Air Fryer Baked Potatoes 45
Garlic Parmesan Carrot Fries 45
Hasselback Potatoes 45
Roasted Maple Dijon Carrots 46
Crispy Smashed Potatoes 46
Jalapeno Popper Stuffed Mushrooms 47
Roasted Beet & Goat Cheese Salad 47
Honey Roasted Parsnip Fries 48

CHAPTER 8: COMFORT FOODS 49

Air Fryer Chicken Pot Pie 49
Mini Deep Dish Chicken Pot Pies 49

- Shepherd's Pie 50
- Air Fryer Pigs in a Blanket 50
- Chicken & Dumplings 51
- Beef & Cheddar Hand Pies 51
- Mac & Cheese Bites 52
- Air Fryer Monte Cristo Sandwiches 52
- Buffalo Chicken Egg Rolls 53
- Crispy Chicken Parmesan 53

CHAPTER 9: DESSERTS 54
- Air Fryer Donuts 54
- Baked Apples with Granola Topping 54
- Lava Cake 55
- Fried Oreos 55
- Baked S'mores Cups 56
- Churro Bites 56
- Pineapple Upside Down Cakes 57
- Red Velvet Lava Crunch Cake 57
- Air Fryer Cookie Cups 58
- Strawberry Hand Pies 58

CHAPTER 10: HOLIDAYS & PARTIES 59
- Spinach Artichoke Dip Bites 59
- Air Fryer Jalapeño Poppers 59
- Pigs in a Blanket Wreath 60
- Thanksgiving Turkey Fryer Sliders 60
- Twice Baked Potato Croquettes 61
- Cranberry Brie Bites 61
- Air Fryer Chicken Wings 62
- Chili Cheese Nachos 62
- Holiday Wreath Bread 63
- Fried Ravioli Skewers 63

CONCLUSION 64

INTRODUCTION

Air frying and toaster ovens have revolutionized the way we cook at home. An air fryer toaster oven is a versatile countertop appliance that combines the functionality of a compact convection oven with the crispy, crunchy abilities of an air fryer. This dynamic duo allows you to air fry, bake, broil, toast, and even dehydrate a variety of foods with little to no oil needed.

At its core, an air fryer toaster oven utilizes rapidly circulating hot air and a compact quartz surface heating element to cook foods from the outside in. The air fryer function works by an internal fan circulating the hot air at high speeds around the food, creating the signature crispy, crunchy texture that mimics deep frying. Tiny droplets of oil rapidly hit the surface of the food and are circulated away before they can fully permeate, resulting in that coveted fried taste and crunch using little to no oil.

The toaster oven function allows you to bake, broil, and toast with radiant heat from heating elements at the top and bottom. This provides more traditional oven like baking and broiling capabilities in a compact size. Many models also include a rotisserie function for roasting meats, dehydrating for making homemade snacks, and even an air fryer mode that combines the convection with the air frying capabilities.

One of the biggest advantages of an air fryer toaster oven is its countertop size. These typically range from a compact 810 inches up to a larger 16inch capacity. This makes them ideal for baking, roasting, air frying, and more for 14 people without heating up a full sized oven. The compact size also means faster preheating and cooking times compared to a traditional oven.

Another major benefit is the health factor. Since air frying uses little to no oil, you can enjoy crispy fried foods with a mere fraction of the calories and fat of deep frying. Air fried french fries, for example, have about 75% less fat and calories than their deep fried counterparts. The toaster oven function also allows you to bake healthier meals and snacks.

When it comes to cooking evenness and quality, air fryer toaster ovens offer a major step up from standard toaster ovens. The strategically angled airflow system and compact quartz surface elements ensure optimal heat circulation with no cold spots or unevenly cooked areas. You'll get evenly browned and crispy results every time.

Cleaning is also a major perk, as most models have dishwasher safe removable trays, racks, baskets, and interiors. This allows for easy cleaning without hours of scrubbing baked on grease.

Using an air fryer toaster oven opens up a world of quick and easy recipes that would otherwise require deep frying or conventional oven cooking. Crispy appetizers like wings, fries, and empanadas? Check. Juicy roasted meats, baked pastas, and dehydrated healthy snacks? This appliance can do it all with little hands-on effort from you.

To get started, all you need to do is add your food to the fryer basket or baking tray, set the desired temperature and function, and let the air fryer toaster oven work its magic. Most models have intuitive digital displays that make setting up a breeze. Shake or toss the contents once or twice during cooking for optimal crispiness.

With its **versatility**, **health advantages**, and **ease of use**, an air fryer toaster oven is a must have for any home kitchen. This cookbook will be your go to guide for mastering this appliance and cooking up quick, delicious, crispy meals with minimal fuss. Get ready to experience fried food bliss without the guilt!

BENEFITS

Air frying offers a trifecta of major benefits that make it one of the hottest cooking trends today health, convenience, and unbeatable versatility. Whether you're looking to cut calories, spend less time in the kitchen, or expand your culinary horizons, an air fryer is your new best friend.

Health Benefits

The primary health benefit of air frying is that it allows you to enjoy your favorite fried foods using little to no oil. Traditional deep frying submerges foods in vat after vat of scalding hot oil, causing them to absorb a shocking amount of fat and calories. An air fryer, on the other hand, requires just a small mist or tossing of oil to achieve that coveted crunchy texture.

In fact, studies have shown that air fried foods have up to 75% less fat and calories compared to the same foods deep fried. This can translate to hundreds of calories shaved off per meal. Air fried french fries, for example, have about 200 calories per serving compared to over 800 for a deep fried serving of the same portion size. Excess oil consumption has also been linked to inflammation, high cholesterol, and weight gain. By drastically reducing the oil, you're doing both your waistline and heart a favor. The air fryer's rapid air circulation also causes foods to retain more nutrients compared to deep frying.

Convenience Benefits

In addition to being healthier, air frying is one of the fastest and most convenient ways to cook. There's no need to wait for large vats of oil to heat up, no splattering to clean up, and no harsh smell lingering in the kitchen. Most air fryers preheat in just 23 minutes, with snacks like chicken wings, fries, and empanadas taking 1525 minutes from start to crispy, golden finish. The compact, countertop size also means no heating up a full sized oven, which saves energy. Air fryers are also incredibly easy to use simply toss your food with a light mist of oil, spread it in the basket, set the temp, and walk away until crunchy perfection is achieved. Many models even have preset programs for popular dishes to take the guesswork out. Air fryers are relatively low maintenance, with dishwasher safe baskets and removable parts for easy cleaning. Their interiors also avoid the grease buildup and stuck on messes of deep fryers. Most simply need a quick wipe down when you're done cooking.

Versatility Benefits

While you may think air fryers are just for making crispy apps and snacks, the truth is they are incredibly versatile. In addition to "frying", an air fryer can bake, roast, reheat, and dehydrate a wide range of dishes to crispy, crunchy perfection with ease.

Use your air fryer to bake up personal pizzas, hand pies, frittatas, and even baked goods like homemade bagels or donuts. It roasts chicken, veggies, and even entire roasts with juicy interiors and crispy exteriors. Dehydrating is also a breeze for making nutrient dense snacks like veggie chips, beef jerky, or dehydrated fruits. In fact, there are entire cookbooks dedicated to air fryer breakfast, dessert, and full meal recipes. As long as you're craving a crispy, evenly cooked result, chances are your air fryer can handle it. This versatility makes it one of the most useful countertop appliances around.

With its speed, ease of use, and ability to make healthier versions of your favorite fried indulgences, it's no wonder that air fryers have become a kitchen staple in recent years. This remarkable appliance has revolutionized home "fried" cooking while saving you time, calories, and mess. From crunchy snacks to crispy mains to guilt free desserts, the air frying possibilities are endless!

OVERVIEW

This ultimate air fryer toaster oven cookbook is your comprehensive guide to mastering one of the most versatile and convenient countertop appliances on the market today. Within these pages, you'll find everything you need to go from an air frying novice to a crispy cuisine expert in no time.

Whether this is your first air fryer toaster oven or you're looking to get more use out of the one you have, this book will empower you with all the knowledge and recipes to truly make the most of it. We'll start with an extensive basics section that leaves no stone unturned when it comes to air fryer toaster oven fundamentals.

You'll learn the precise workings of the different functions like air fry, bake, broil, dehydrate and more. We'll cover all the accessories that can help you expand your capabilities, from bacon presses and rotisserie kits to pizza and dehydrating racks. You'll also get detailed guidance on making the switch from traditional recipes by understanding air fry times, temperatures, and top tips for crispy perfection every time.

From there, we'll dive into over 100 thoroughly tested recipes exclusively designed for the air fryer toaster oven. These recipes go way beyond just snacks and apps you'll find entire chapters on complete meals, vegetarian mains, roasted meats and seafood, baked pastas and pizzas, sides, and even decadent desserts, all crafted to be cooked with ease in your air fryer oven. Each recipe is masterfully developed to deliver maximum crunch, moisture, and flavor in every bite using a minimum of oil and energy resources. From cheesy baked pastas and hand pies to juicy roast chicken and dehydrated snacks, you'll be amazed at the range and quality that can come from this space saving appliance.

For ease of use, every recipe has a detailed, straightforward ingredients list and step by step instructions that assume no prior air frying knowledge. You'll also find make ahead, meal prep, and storage guidance, as well as built-in tips and tricks for optimum results no matter your skill level.

To help balance it all out, we've included calorie counts, nutrition breakdowns, and handy labels to call out vegetarian, gluten-free, keto-friendly, and more with a quick glance. You'll even find creative ways to repurpose leftovers into new fast and fresh meals.

As a special bonus, we've included entire chapters dedicated to meal prep, food planning, and stocking your air fryer toaster pantry. Following the plans and shopping lists in this section, you'll always have the right ingredients on hand to whip up fast, satisfying meals in your air fryer with no last-minute grocery runs.

This book is designed to be your comprehensive air fryer toaster oven resource for years to come. The lay-flat binding and thick, unbendable pages ensure durability through many cooking adventures. You can easily wipe away any splatters or spills to keep it crisp as new.

No matter your dietary needs, schedule, or skill level, you'll find an abundance of recipes to satisfy every craving while streamlining your kitchen routine. With this book in hand, you'll maximize the versatility of your air fryer toaster oven like never before through fast, easy, and healthy meals.

So get ready to experience the revolutionary crispy power of air frying meets countertop oven convenience! **Your world of cooking is about to get a whole lot crunchier.**

CHAPTER 1: APPETIZERS & SNACKS

Crispy Air Fryer Chickpeas

Prep: 5 mins | Cook: 20 mins | Serves: 4
Ingredients:
- US: 400g canned chickpeas (drained and rinsed), 15ml olive oil, 1 teaspoon paprika, 1 teaspoon garlic powder, salt, pepper
- UK: 400g canned chickpeas (drained and rinsed), 15ml olive oil, 1 teaspoon paprika, 1 teaspoon garlic powder, salt, pepper

Instructions:
1. Preheat your air fryer toaster oven to 200°C (400°F).
2. In a bowl, toss chickpeas with olive oil, paprika, garlic powder, salt, and pepper until evenly coated.
3. Spread the seasoned chickpeas in the air fryer basket in a single layer.
4. Air fry for about 20 minutes, shaking the basket halfway through, until chickpeas are crispy.
5. Once done, remove the chickpeas from the air fryer and let them cool slightly before serving.
6. Enjoy the Crispy Air Fryer Chickpeas as a crunchy snack or a topping for salads!

Nutritional Info (per serving): Calories: 140 | Fat: 5g | Carbs: 18g | Protein: 6g

Veggie Fritters with Yogurt Dip

Prep: 15 mins | Cook: 15 mins | Serves: 4
Ingredients:
- US: 2 medium zucchinis (grated and excess moisture squeezed out), 1 medium carrot (grated), 1/2 small red onion (finely chopped), 2 eggs, 60g allpurpose flour, 30g grated Parmesan cheese, salt, pepper, 120g Greek yogurt, 1 tablespoon lemon juice, chopped fresh dill (for garnish)
- UK: 2 medium zucchinis (grated and excess moisture squeezed out), 1 medium carrot (grated), 1/2 small red onion (finely chopped), 2 eggs, 60g allpurpose flour, 30g grated Parmesan cheese, salt, pepper, 120g Greek yogurt, 1 tablespoon lemon juice, chopped fresh dill (for garnish)

Instructions:
1. Preheat your air fryer toaster oven to 200°C (400°F).
2. In a large bowl, combine grated zucchini, carrot, red onion, eggs, flour, Parmesan cheese, salt, and pepper.
3. Mix until well combined to form a batter.
4. Scoop tablespoonsful of the batter and shape into fritters.
5. Place the fritters in the air fryer basket in a single layer, ensuring they are not touching.

6. Air fry for about 15 minutes, flipping halfway through, until fritters are golden brown and crispy.
7. In a small bowl, mix Greek yogurt with lemon juice to make the dip.
8. Garnish the fritters with chopped fresh dill and serve hot with the yogurt dip on the side.

Nutritional Info (per serving): Calories: 180 | Fat: 6g | Carbs: 22g | Protein: 10g

Coconut Shrimp with Sweet Chili Sauce

Prep: 20 mins | Cook: 10 mins | Serves: 4

Ingredients:
- US: 400g large shrimp (peeled and deveined), 100g shredded coconut, 60g breadcrumbs, 2 eggs (beaten), salt, pepper, cooking spray, sweet chili sauce (for dipping)
- UK: 400g large shrimp (peeled and deveined), 100g shredded coconut, 60g breadcrumbs, 2 eggs (beaten), salt, pepper, cooking spray, sweet chili sauce (for dipping)

Instructions:
1. Preheat your air fryer toaster oven to 200°C (400°F).
2. In separate bowls, place beaten eggs, shredded coconut mixed with breadcrumbs, and seasoned flour.
3. Dip each shrimp in flour, then egg, and finally coat with the coconut breadcrumb mixture.
4. Place the coated shrimp in the air fryer basket in a single layer.
5. Lightly spray the shrimp with cooking spray.
6. Air fry for about 10 minutes, flipping halfway through, until shrimp are golden brown and cooked through.
7. Once done, serve the Coconut Shrimp hot with sweet chili sauce for dipping.

Nutritional Info (per serving): Calories: 280 | Fat: 12g | Carbs: 20g | Protein: 20g

Air Fryer Blooming Onion

Prep: 15 mins | Cook: 20 mins | Serves: 4

Ingredients:
- US: 1 large onion, 120g allpurpose flour, 2 eggs (beaten), 100g breadcrumbs, 1 teaspoon paprika, 1 teaspoon garlic powder, salt, pepper, cooking spray, blooming onion dipping sauce (optional)
- UK: 1 large onion, 120g allpurpose flour, 2 eggs (beaten), 100g breadcrumbs, 1 teaspoon paprika, 1 teaspoon garlic powder, salt, pepper, cooking spray, blooming onion dipping sauce (optional)

Instructions:
1. Preheat your air fryer toaster oven to 200°C (400°F).
2. Cut the top of the onion off and peel the skin, leaving the root intact. Slice the onion vertically into sections, stopping about 1/2 inch from the root end.
3. Gently spread the onion layers apart to resemble a blooming flower.

4. In separate bowls, place flour, beaten eggs, and a mixture of breadcrumbs, paprika, garlic powder, salt, and pepper.
5. Dredge the onion in flour, then dip into the beaten eggs, and finally coat with the breadcrumb mixture, ensuring to get in between the layers.
6. Place the coated onion in the air fryer basket, root side down.
7. Lightly spray the onion with cooking spray.
8. Air fry for about 20 minutes, until the onion is golden brown and crispy.
9. Serve the Air Fryer Blooming Onion hot with your favorite dipping sauce, like blooming onion sauce or chipotle mayo.

Nutritional Info (per serving): Calories: 220 | Fat: 5g | Carbs: 38g | Protein: 7g

Spicy Buffalo Cauliflower Bites

Prep: 10 mins | Cook: 20 mins | Serves: 4

Ingredients:
- US: 1 medium head cauliflower (cut into florets), 60g allpurpose flour, 120ml milk, 1 teaspoon garlic powder, 1 teaspoon paprika, 120ml buffalo sauce, 30g melted butter, salt, pepper, ranch or blue cheese dressing (for dipping)
- UK: 1 medium head cauliflower (cut into florets), 60g allpurpose flour, 120ml milk, 1 teaspoon garlic powder, 1 teaspoon paprika, 120ml buffalo sauce, 30g melted butter, salt, pepper, ranch or blue cheese dressing (for dipping)

Instructions:
1. Preheat your air fryer toaster oven to 200°C (400°F).
2. In a bowl, whisk together flour, milk, garlic powder, paprika, salt, and pepper to make a batter.
3. Dip cauliflower florets into the batter, shaking off any excess.
4. Place the battered cauliflower in the air fryer basket in a single layer.
5. Air fry for about 20 minutes, shaking the basket halfway through, until cauliflower is crispy and golden brown.
6. In a separate bowl, mix buffalo sauce with melted butter.
7. Once cauliflower is cooked, toss it in the spicy buffalo sauce mixture until evenly coated.
8. Serve the Spicy Buffalo Cauliflower Bites hot with ranch or blue cheese dressing for dipping.

Nutritional Info (per serving): Calories: 180 | Fat: 9g | Carbs: 20g | Protein: 5g

Loaded Air Fryer Nachos

Prep: 10 mins | Cook: 10 mins | Serves: 4

Ingredients:
- US: 200g tortilla chips, 200g shredded cheddar cheese, 200g cooked black beans, 100g diced tomatoes, 100g diced red onion, 100g sliced jalapenos, 100g sliced black olives, 100g sour cream, chopped fresh cilantro (for garnish)

- UK: 200g tortilla chips, 200g shredded cheddar cheese, 200g cooked black beans, 100g diced tomatoes, 100g diced red onion, 100g sliced jalapenos, 100g sliced black olives, 100g sour cream, chopped fresh cilantro (for garnish)

Instructions:
1. Preheat your air fryer toaster oven to 180°C (350°F).
2. Arrange tortilla chips on the air fryer basket in a single layer.
3. Sprinkle shredded cheddar cheese evenly over the tortilla chips.
4. Top with cooked black beans, diced tomatoes, diced red onion, sliced jalapenos, and sliced black olives.
5. Air fry for about 10 minutes, until the cheese is melted and bubbly.
6. Once done, remove the loaded nachos from the air fryer.
7. Drizzle with sour cream and garnish with chopped fresh cilantro.
8. Serve the Loaded Air Fryer Nachos immediately as a crowd pleasing appetizer or snack!

Nutritional Info (per serving): Calories: 450 | Fat: 25g | Carbs: 45g | Protein: 15g

Crispy Avocado Fries

Prep: 15 mins | Cook: 10 mins | Serves: 4

Ingredients:
- US: 2 ripe avocados (peeled, pitted, and sliced), 60g allpurpose flour, 2 eggs (beaten), 100g breadcrumbs, 1 teaspoon garlic powder, 1 teaspoon paprika, salt, pepper, cooking spray, sriracha mayo (for dipping)
- UK: 2 ripe avocados (peeled, pitted, and sliced), 60g allpurpose flour, 2 eggs (beaten), 100g breadcrumbs, 1 teaspoon garlic powder, 1 teaspoon paprika, salt, pepper, cooking spray, sriracha mayo (for dipping)

Instructions:
1. Preheat your air fryer toaster oven to 200°C (400°F).
2. In separate bowls, place flour, beaten eggs, and a mixture of breadcrumbs, garlic powder, paprika, salt, and pepper.
3. Dredge avocado slices in flour, then dip into the beaten eggs, and finally coat with the breadcrumb mixture.
4. Place the coated avocado slices in the air fryer basket in a single layer.
5. Lightly spray the avocado fries with cooking spray.
6. Air fry for about 10 minutes, flipping halfway through, until golden brown and crispy.
7. Serve the Crispy Avocado Fries hot with sriracha mayo for dipping.

Nutritional Info (per serving): Calories: 220 | Fat: 12g | Carbs: 24g | Protein: 6g

Bacon Wrapped Tater Tots

Prep: 10 mins | Cook: 20 mins | Serves: 4

Ingredients:
- US: 400g frozen tater tots, 8 slices bacon, salt, pepper, maple syrup (for dipping)
- UK: 400g frozen tater tots, 8 slices bacon, salt, pepper, maple syrup (for dipping)

Instructions:
1. Preheat your air fryer toaster oven to 200°C (400°F).
2. Wrap each tater tot with a slice of bacon.
3. Secure the bacon with toothpicks if needed.
4. Place the bacon wrapped tater tots in the air fryer basket in a single layer.
5. Season with salt and pepper.
6. Air fry for about 20 minutes, flipping halfway through, until bacon is crispy and tater tots are golden brown.
7. Once cooked, remove the bacon wrapped tater tots from the air fryer and let them cool slightly.
8. Serve the Bacon Wrapped Tater Tots hot with maple syrup for dipping.

Nutritional Info (per serving): Calories: 300 | Fat: 18g | Carbs: 22g | Protein: 10g

Pesto Stuffed Mushrooms

Prep: 15 mins | Cook: 15 mins | Serves: 4

Ingredients:
- US: 12 large mushrooms, 60g pesto sauce, 60g shredded mozzarella cheese, 30g grated Parmesan cheese, salt, pepper, chopped fresh basil (for garnish)
- UK: 12 large mushrooms, 60g pesto sauce, 60g shredded mozzarella cheese, 30g grated Parmesan cheese, salt, pepper, chopped fresh basil (for garnish)

Instructions:
1. Preheat your air fryer toaster oven to 180°C (350°F).
2. Remove the stems from the mushrooms and discard.
3. Fill each mushroom cap with pesto sauce.
4. Top with shredded mozzarella cheese and grated Parmesan cheese.
5. Season with salt and pepper.
6. Place the stuffed mushrooms in the air fryer basket in a single layer.
7. Air fry for about 15 minutes, until cheese is melted and mushrooms are tender.
8. Once cooked, garnish the Pesto Stuffed Mushrooms with chopped fresh basil before serving.

Nutritional Info (per serving): Calories: 120 | Fat: 8g | Carbs: 6g | Protein: 5g

Churro Bites

Prep: 20 mins | Cook: 10 mins | Serves: 4

Ingredients:
- US: 1 sheet puff pastry, 60g unsalted butter (melted), 50g granulated sugar, 1 teaspoon ground cinnamon, chocolate sauce (for dipping)
- UK: 1 sheet puff pastry, 60g unsalted butter (melted), 50g granulated sugar, 1 teaspoon ground cinnamon, chocolate sauce (for dipping)

Instructions:
1. Preheat your air fryer toaster oven to 180°C (350°F).
2. Roll out puff pastry and brush with melted butter.
3. In a bowl, mix together granulated sugar and ground cinnamon.
4. Sprinkle the cinnamon sugar mixture evenly over the puff pastry.
5. Cut the pastry into small squares or strips.
6. Place the churro bites in the air fryer basket in a single layer.
7. Air fry for about 10 minutes, until golden brown and crispy.
8. Once cooked, remove the churro bites from the air fryer and let them cool slightly.
9. Serve the Churro Bites warm with chocolate sauce for dipping.

Nutritional Info (per serving): Calories: 320 | Fat: 18g | Carbs: 36g | Protein: 4g

CHAPTER 2: BREAKFAST & BRUNCH

Air Fryer Bacon & Egg Cups

Prep: 10 mins | Cook: 12 mins | Serves: 4

Ingredients:
- US: 8 slices bacon, 8 large eggs, salt, pepper, chopped chives (for garnish)
- UK: 8 slices streaky bacon, 8 large eggs, salt, pepper, chopped chives (for garnish)

Instructions:
1. Preheat your air fryer to 180°C (350°F).
2. Line each cup of a muffin tin with a slice of bacon, forming a cup shape.
3. Crack an egg into each bacon cup. Season with salt and pepper.
4. Place the muffin tin in the air fryer basket.
5. Air fry for about 10-12 minutes until the egg whites are set and the bacon is crispy.
6. Garnish with chopped chives before serving.

Nutritional Info: Calories: 220 | Fat: 15g | Carbs: 1g | Protein: 18g

Overnight Cinnamon Rolls

Prep: 20 mins | Cook: 15 mins | Serves: 8 rolls

Ingredients:
- US: 500g refrigerated cinnamon roll dough, 60g butter (softened), 100g brown sugar, 1 tablespoon ground cinnamon, 100g cream cheese (for icing)
- UK: 500g refrigerated cinnamon roll dough, 60g butter (softened), 100g light brown soft sugar, 1 tablespoon ground cinnamon, 100g cream cheese (for icing)

Instructions:
1. Grease the air fryer basket or tray.
2. Roll out the cinnamon roll dough into a rectangle.
3. Spread softened butter over the dough, then sprinkle with brown sugar and cinnamon.
4. Roll up the dough tightly, then slice into 8 rolls.
5. Place the rolls in the air fryer basket, leaving space between each roll.
6. Air fry at 160°C (320°F) for 12-15 minutes until golden brown.
7. Allow the rolls to cool slightly before icing with cream cheese frosting.

Nutritional Info: Calories: 280 | Fat: 15g | Carbs: 33g | Protein: 3g

Hash Brown Breakfast Casserole

Prep: 15 mins | Cook: 25 mins | Serves: 6

Ingredients:
- US: 500g frozen hash browns, 200g diced ham, 1 bell pepper (diced), 1 onion (diced), 200g shredded cheddar cheese, 6 large eggs, 240ml milk, salt, pepper

- UK: 500g frozen hash browns, 200g diced ham, 1 bell pepper (diced), 1 onion (diced), 200g grated cheddar cheese, 6 large eggs, 240ml milk, salt, pepper

Instructions:
1. In a large bowl, mix together hash browns, diced ham, bell pepper, onion, and shredded cheese.
2. In another bowl, whisk together eggs, milk, salt, and pepper.
3. Pour the egg mixture over the hash brown mixture and stir to combine.
4. Transfer the mixture to an air fryersafe casserole dish.
5. Air fry at 180°C (350°F) for 2025 minutes until the eggs are set and the top is golden brown.
6. Let it cool slightly before serving.

Nutritional Info: Calories: 320 | Fat: 18g | Carbs: 22g | Protein: 18g

Frittata Muffins with Spinach & Feta

Prep: 15 mins | Cook: 15 mins | Serves: 6 muffins

Ingredients:
- US: 6 large eggs, 60ml milk, 50g baby spinach (chopped), 50g crumbled feta cheese, salt, pepper
- UK: 6 large eggs, 60ml milk, 50g baby spinach (chopped), 50g crumbled feta cheese, salt, pepper

Instructions:
1. In a bowl, whisk together eggs, milk, salt, and pepper.
2. Stir in chopped spinach and crumbled feta.
3. Divide the mixture evenly among greased muffin cups.
4. Air fry at 180°C (350°F) for 1215 minutes until set.
5. Allow to cool slightly before removing from the muffin tin.

Nutritional Info: Calories: 110 | Fat: 7g | Carbs: 2g | Protein: 8g

Air Fryer Doughnuts

Prep: 15 mins | Cook: 10 mins | Serves: 8 doughnuts

Ingredients:
- US: 250g refrigerated biscuit dough, 50g melted butter, 100g granulated sugar, 1 tablespoon ground cinnamon
- UK: 250g refrigerated biscuit dough, 50g melted butter, 100g caster sugar, 1 tablespoon ground cinnamon

Instructions:
1. Flatten biscuit dough and cut out rounds with a doughnut cutter.
2. Brush both sides of each doughnut with melted butter.
3. Place doughnuts in the air fryer basket in a single layer.
4. Air fry at 180°C (350°F) for 810 minutes until golden brown.
5. Mix sugar and cinnamon in a bowl. Dip each doughnut in the mixture to coat.
6. Serve warm.

Nutritional Info: Calories: 180 | Fat: 8g | Carbs: 26g | Protein: 2g

Breakfast Sausage Patties

Prep: 10 mins | Cook: 15 mins | Serves: 4 patties
Ingredients:
- US: 400g ground pork, 1 teaspoon salt, 1 teaspoon ground black pepper, 1/2 teaspoon dried sage, 1/2 teaspoon dried thyme, 1/2 teaspoon dried rosemary
- UK: 400g pork mince, 1 teaspoon salt, 1 teaspoon ground black pepper, 1/2 teaspoon dried sage, 1/2 teaspoon dried thyme, 1/2 teaspoon dried rosemary

Instructions:
1. In a bowl, mix together ground pork, salt, pepper, and herbs.
2. Divide the mixture into 4 portions and shape into patties.
3. Preheat the air fryer to 180°C (350°F).
4. Place the patties in the air fryer basket.
5. Air fry for 12-15 minutes, flipping halfway through, until cooked through.
6. Serve hot with your favorite breakfast sides.

Nutritional Info: Calories: 220 | Fat: 15g | Carbs: 1g | Protein: 20g

French Toast Sticks

Prep: 10 mins | Cook: 10 mins | Serves: 4
Ingredients:
- US: 4 slices bread, 2 large eggs, 60ml milk, 1 teaspoon vanilla extract, 1/2 teaspoon ground cinnamon, maple syrup (for serving)
- UK: 4 slices bread, 2 large eggs, 60ml milk, 1 teaspoon vanilla extract, 1/2 teaspoon ground cinnamon, maple syrup (for serving)

Instructions:
1. Cut each slice of bread into strips to make sticks.
2. In a shallow dish, whisk together eggs, milk, vanilla, and cinnamon.
3. Dip each bread stick into the egg mixture, coating evenly.
4. Preheat the air fryer to 180°C (350°F).
5. Place the French toast sticks in the air fryer basket.
6. Air fry for 8-10 minutes until golden brown and crispy.
7. Serve with maple syrup for dipping.

Nutritional Info: Calories: 180 | Fat: 5g | Carbs: 26g | Protein: 7g

Mini Quiches

Prep: 15 mins | Cook: 15 mins | Serves: 6 mini quiches
Ingredients:
- US: 1 refrigerated pie crust, 3 large eggs, 120ml milk, 50g shredded cheddar cheese, 50g diced ham, 1/4 cup diced bell pepper, salt, pepper

- UK: 1 refrigerated shortcrust pastry, 3 large eggs, 120ml milk, 50g grated cheddar cheese, 50g diced ham, 1/4 cup diced bell pepper, salt, pepper

Instructions:
1. Roll out the pie crust and cut into circles to fit your muffin tin.
2. Press the pie crust circles into greased muffin cups.
3. In a bowl, whisk together eggs, milk, salt, and pepper.
4. Stir in cheese, ham, and bell pepper.
5. Pour the egg mixture into the pie crust cups.
6. Preheat the air fryer to 180°C (350°F).
7. Air fry for 12-15 minutes until set and golden brown.
8. Allow to cool slightly before serving.

Nutritional Info: Calories: 220 | Fat: 12g | Carbs: 18g | Protein: 10g

Home Fries

Prep: 10 mins | Cook: 20 mins | Serves: 4

Ingredients:
- US: 500g potatoes (cubed), 30ml olive oil, 1 teaspoon paprika, 1/2 teaspoon garlic powder, salt, pepper
- UK: 500g potatoes (cubed), 30ml olive oil, 1 teaspoon paprika, 1/2 teaspoon garlic powder, salt, pepper

Instructions:
1. In a bowl, toss potatoes with olive oil, paprika, garlic powder, salt, and pepper.
2. Preheat the air fryer to 200°C (400°F).
3. Spread the seasoned potatoes in the air fryer basket in a single layer.
4. Air fry for 15-20 minutes, shaking the basket halfway through, until golden and crispy.
5. Serve hot as a side dish for breakfast.

Nutritional Info: Calories: 180 | Fat: 7g | Carbs: 28g | Protein: 3g

Air Fryer Breakfast Burritos

Prep: 15 mins | Cook: 10 mins | Serves: 4 burritos

Ingredients:
- US: 4 large flour tortillas, 4 large eggs, 60ml milk, 100g diced ham, 50g shredded cheddar cheese, 1/4 cup diced bell pepper, salt, pepper, salsa (for serving)
- UK: 4 large flour tortillas, 4 large eggs, 60ml milk, 100g diced ham, 50g grated cheddar cheese, 1/4 cup diced bell pepper, salt, pepper, salsa (for serving)

Instructions:
1. In a bowl, whisk together eggs, milk, salt, and pepper.
2. Scramble the eggs in a pan until just set.
3. Lay out tortillas and divide scrambled eggs, diced ham, cheese, and bell pepper among them.
4. Fold in the sides of each tortilla, then roll up tightly into burritos.

5. Preheat the air fryer to 180°C (350°F).
6. Place the burritos in the air fryer basket seam side down.
7. Air fry for 8-10 minutes until golden and crispy.
8. Serve with salsa for dipping.

Nutritional Info: Calories: 320 | Fat: 15g | Carbs: 30g | Protein: 17g

CHAPTER 3: VEGETARIAN MAINS

Black Bean & Quinoa Burgers
Prep: 15 mins | Cook: 20 mins | Serves: 4
Ingredients:
- US: 1 can (400g) black beans, drained and rinsed; 100g cooked quinoa; 1/2 onion, finely chopped; 2 cloves garlic, minced; 1 teaspoon cumin; 1 teaspoon paprika; salt and pepper to taste; 30g breadcrumbs; 1 tablespoon olive oil
- UK: 1 can (400g) black beans, drained and rinsed; 100g cooked quinoa; 1/2 onion, finely chopped; 2 cloves garlic, minced; 1 teaspoon cumin; 1 teaspoon paprika; salt and pepper to taste; 30g breadcrumbs; 1 tablespoon olive oil

Instructions:
1. Mash black beans in a bowl.
2. Add quinoa, onion, garlic, cumin, paprika, salt, pepper, and breadcrumbs. Mix well.
3. Form mixture into patties.
4. Preheat air fryer toaster oven to 180°C.
5. Brush patties with olive oil.
6. Cook for 10 minutes, flip, and cook for another 10 minutes until golden brown.
7. Serve on buns with desired toppings.

Nutritional Info (per serving): Calories: 220 | Fat: 4g | Carbs: 34g | Protein: 11g

Cauliflower Buffalo Bites
Prep: 15 mins | Cook: 20 mins | Serves: 4
Ingredients:
- US: 1 medium cauliflower, cut into florets; 60g flour; 60ml water; 60ml hot sauce; 30g melted butter; 1 teaspoon garlic powder; 1/2 teaspoon paprika; salt and pepper to taste
- UK: 1 medium cauliflower, cut into florets; 60g flour; 60ml water; 60ml hot sauce; 30g melted butter; 1 teaspoon garlic powder; 1/2 teaspoon paprika; salt and pepper to taste

Instructions:
1. In a bowl, mix flour, water, hot sauce, melted butter, garlic powder, paprika, salt, and pepper to make the batter.
2. Dip cauliflower florets in the batter, ensuring they are coated evenly.
3. Preheat air fryer toaster oven to 200°C.
4. Place cauliflower on the air fryer basket in a single layer.
5. Cook for 10 minutes, flip, and cook for another 10 minutes until crispy.
6. Serve with ranch or blue cheese dressing.

Nutritional Info (per serving): Calories: 150 | Fat: 8g | Carbs: 18g | Protein: 5g

Crispy Air Fryer Falafel

Prep: 15 mins | Cook: 15 mins | Serves: 4

Ingredients:
- US: 1 can (400g) chickpeas, drained and rinsed; 1/2 onion, chopped; 2 cloves garlic; 30g fresh parsley; 1 teaspoon cumin; 1 teaspoon coriander; 1/2 teaspoon baking powder; salt and pepper to taste; 30ml olive oil
- UK: 1 can (400g) chickpeas, drained and rinsed; 1/2 onion, chopped; 2 cloves garlic; 30g fresh parsley; 1 teaspoon cumin; 1 teaspoon coriander; 1/2 teaspoon baking powder; salt and pepper to taste; 30ml olive oil

Instructions:
1. In a food processor, blend chickpeas, onion, garlic, parsley, cumin, coriander, baking powder, salt, and pepper until smooth.
2. Form mixture into balls and flatten slightly.
3. Preheat air fryer toaster oven to 180°C.
4. Brush falafel with olive oil.
5. Cook for 10 minutes, flip, and cook for another 5 minutes until golden brown.
6. Serve with hummus and pita bread.

Nutritional Info (per serving): Calories: 180 | Fat: 7g | Carbs: 24g | Protein: 6g

Baked Stuffed Tomatoes

Prep: 15 mins | Cook: 25 mins | Serves: 4

Ingredients:
- US: 4 large tomatoes; 100g cooked quinoa; 60g feta cheese, crumbled; 1/2 onion, finely chopped; 2 cloves garlic, minced; 30g fresh parsley, chopped; salt and pepper to taste; olive oil for drizzling
- UK: 4 large tomatoes; 100g cooked quinoa; 60g feta cheese, crumbled; 1/2 onion, finely chopped; 2 cloves garlic, minced; 30g fresh parsley, chopped; salt and pepper to taste; olive oil for drizzling

Instructions:
1. Cut the tops off the tomatoes and scoop out the insides.
2. In a bowl, mix quinoa, feta cheese, onion, garlic, parsley, salt, and pepper.
3. Stuff the tomatoes with the quinoa mixture.
4. Preheat air fryer toaster oven to 180°C.
5. Drizzle stuffed tomatoes with olive oil.
6. Bake for 2025 minutes until tomatoes are softened.
7. Serve as a side dish or light lunch.

Nutritional Info (per serving): Calories: 140 | Fat: 5g | Carbs: 18g | Protein: 6g

Vegetable Pakoras

Prep: 15 mins | Cook: 15 mins | Serves: 4

Ingredients:
- US: 1 small potato, peeled and grated; 1 small onion, finely chopped; 1 small carrot, grated; 60g peas; 60g cauliflower florets, chopped; 60g spinach, chopped; 60g chickpea flour; 1 teaspoon cumin; 1 teaspoon garam masala; 1/2 teaspoon turmeric; 1/2 teaspoon chili powder; salt to taste; water as needed; oil for frying
- UK: 1 small potato, peeled and grated; 1 small onion, finely chopped; 1 small carrot, grated; 60g peas; 60g cauliflower florets, chopped; 60g spinach, chopped; 60g chickpea flour; 1 teaspoon cumin; 1 teaspoon garam masala; 1/2 teaspoon turmeric; 1/2 teaspoon chili powder; salt to taste; water as needed; oil for frying

Instructions:
1. In a bowl, mix all vegetables, chickpea flour, cumin, garam masala, turmeric, chili powder, and salt.
2. Add water gradually to make a thick batter.
3. Preheat air fryer toaster oven to 180°C.
4. Drop spoonfuls of batter into the air fryer basket.
5. Cook for 10 minutes, flip, and cook for another 5minutes until golden brown.
6. Serve hot with chutney or yogurt sauce.

Nutritional Info (per serving): Calories: 180 | Fat: 4g | Carbs: 30g | Protein: 6g

Mediterranean Stuffed Peppers

Prep: 20 mins | Cook: 25 mins | Serves: 4

Ingredients:
- US: 4 bell peppers; 100g cooked quinoa; 60g cherry tomatoes, halved; 60g feta cheese, crumbled; 1/2 onion, finely chopped; 2 cloves garlic, minced; 30g black olives, chopped; 30g fresh parsley, chopped; salt and pepper to taste; olive oil for drizzling
- UK: 4 bell peppers; 100g cooked quinoa; 60g cherry tomatoes, halved; 60g feta cheese, crumbled; 1/2 onion, finely chopped; 2 cloves garlic, minced; 30g black olives, chopped; 30g fresh parsley, chopped; salt and pepper to taste; olive oil for drizzling

Instructions:
1. Cut the tops off the peppers and remove seeds.
2. In a bowl, mix quinoa, cherry tomatoes, feta cheese, onion, garlic, olives, parsley, salt, and pepper.
3. Stuff the peppers with the quinoa mixture.
4. Preheat air fryer toaster oven to 180°C.
5. Drizzle stuffed peppers with olive oil.
6. Bake for 2025 minutes until peppers are softened.
7. Serve as a hearty vegetarian main.

Nutritional Info (per serving): Calories: 160 | Fat: 5g | Carbs: 22g | Protein: 7g

Butternut Squash & Kale Quesadillas
Prep: 15 mins | Cook: 20 mins | Serves: 4
Ingredients:
- US: 400g butternut squash, peeled and cubed; 60g kale, chopped; 1/2 onion, finely chopped; 2 cloves garlic, minced; 1 teaspoon cumin; 1 teaspoon chili powder; salt and pepper to taste; 4 large tortillas; 120g shredded cheese (cheddar or mozzarella); olive oil for brushing
- UK: 400g butternut squash, peeled and cubed; 60g kale, chopped; 1/2 onion, finely chopped; 2 cloves garlic, minced; 1 teaspoon cumin; 1 teaspoon chili powder; salt and pepper to taste; 4 large tortillas; 120g shredded cheese (cheddar or mozzarella); olive oil for brushing

Instructions:
1. In a skillet, sauté butternut squash, kale, onion, garlic, cumin, chili powder, salt, and pepper until tender.
2. Place a tortilla on a flat surface.
3. Spread butternut squash mixture and cheese evenly on one half of the tortilla.
4. Fold the tortilla in half to cover the filling.
5. Preheat air fryer toaster oven to 180°C.
6. Brush both sides of the quesadilla with olive oil.
7. Cook for 10 minutes, flip, and cook for another 57 minutes until crispy.
8. Serve with salsa and sour cream.

Nutritional Info (per serving): Calories: 290 | Fat: 12g | Carbs: 36g | Protein: 10g

Lentil Sloppy Joes
Prep: 15 mins | Cook: 25 mins | Serves: 4
Ingredients:
- US: 200g brown lentils, cooked; 1/2 onion, finely chopped; 1/2 bell pepper, finely chopped; 2 cloves garlic, minced; 240ml tomato sauce; 2 tablespoons tomato paste; 1 tablespoon maple syrup; 1 tablespoon Worcestershire sauce; 1 teaspoon mustard; salt and pepper to taste; 4 burger buns
- UK: 200g brown lentils, cooked; 1/2 onion, finely chopped; 1/2 bell pepper, finely chopped; 2 cloves garlic, minced; 240ml tomato sauce; 2 tablespoons tomato paste; 1 tablespoon maple syrup; 1 tablespoon Worcestershire sauce; 1 teaspoon mustard; salt and pepper to taste; 4 burger buns

Instructions:
1. In a skillet, sauté onion, bell pepper, and garlic until soft.
2. Add cooked lentils, tomato sauce, tomato paste, maple syrup, Worcestershire sauce, mustard, salt, and pepper. Stir well.
3. Simmer for 1015 minutes until the mixture thickens.
4. Preheat air fryer toaster oven to 180°C.

5. Toast burger buns in the oven for 35 minutes until lightly browned.
6. Spoon lentil mixture onto toasted buns.
7. Serve hot as a comforting meal.

Nutritional Info (per serving): Calories: 320 | Fat: 2g | Carbs: 62g | Protein: 14g

Baked Veggie Egg Rolls

Prep: 20 mins | Cook: 20 mins | Serves: 4

Ingredients:
- US: 8 egg roll wrappers; 200g coleslaw mix; 100g mushrooms, chopped; 1/2 onion, finely chopped; 2 cloves garlic, minced; 30g bean sprouts; 30ml soy sauce; 1 teaspoon sesame oil; salt and pepper to taste; olive oil for brushing
- UK: 8 egg roll wrappers; 200g coleslaw mix; 100g mushrooms, chopped; 1/2 onion, finely chopped; 2 cloves garlic, minced; 30g bean sprouts; 30ml soy sauce; 1 teaspoon sesame oil; salt and pepper to taste; olive oil for brushing

Instructions:
1. In a skillet, sauté mushrooms, onion, and garlic until tender.
2. Add coleslaw mix, bean sprouts, soy sauce, sesame oil, salt, and pepper. Cook for another 23 minutes.
3. Place a spoonful of the vegetable mixture onto each egg roll wrapper.
4. Roll tightly, tucking in the sides, and seal the edges with water.
5. Preheat air fryer toaster oven to 180°C.
6. Brush egg rolls with olive oil.
7. Cook for 10 minutes, flip, and cook for another 10 minutes until golden brown.
8. Serve with sweet chili sauce for dipping.

Nutritional Info (per serving): Calories: 220 | Fat: 5g | Carbs: 38g | Protein: 6g

BBQ Jackfruit Sandwiches

Prep: 15 mins | Cook: 25 mins | Serves: 4

Ingredients:
- US: 400g canned young jackfruit, drained and shredded; 240ml barbecue sauce; 4 burger buns; 1/4 red cabbage, thinly sliced; 1/4 cup vegan mayonnaise; 1 tablespoon apple cider vinegar; salt and pepper to taste
- UK: 400g canned young jackfruit, drained and shredded; 240ml barbecue sauce; 4 burger buns; 1/4 red cabbage, thinly sliced; 1/4 cup vegan mayonnaise; 1 tablespoon apple cider vinegar; salt and pepper to taste

Instructions:
1. In a skillet, cook shredded jackfruit with barbecue sauce until heated through.
2. In a bowl, mix red cabbage, vegan mayonnaise, apple cider vinegar, salt, and pepper to make coleslaw.
3. Toast burger buns in the air fryer toaster oven for 35 minutes.

4. Assemble sandwiches with BBQ jackfruit and coleslaw.
5. Serve hot as a tasty vegan alternative.

Nutritional Info (per serving): Calories: 340 | Fat: 7g | Carbs: 64g | Protein: 5g

CHAPTER 4: MEAT & POULTRY

Perfect Air Fryer Steak

Prep: 10 mins | Cook: 12 mins | Serves: 2

Ingredients:
- US: 2 ribeye steaks (200g each), 15ml olive oil, 2 cloves garlic (minced), 1 teaspoon dried thyme, salt, pepper
- UK: 2 ribeye steaks (200g each), 15ml olive oil, 2 cloves garlic (minced), 1 teaspoon dried thyme, salt, pepper

Instructions:
1. Preheat your air fryer toaster oven to 200°C (400°F).
2. Rub both sides of the steaks with olive oil, minced garlic, dried thyme, salt, and pepper.
3. Place the steaks in the air fryer basket in a single layer.
4. Air fry for about 6 minutes, then flip the steaks.
5. Air fry for another 6 minutes for medium rare doneness.
6. Adjust cooking time according to desired doneness.
7. Once done, let the steaks rest for a few minutes before slicing.
8. Serve the Perfect Air Fryer Steak hot with your favorite sides.

Nutritional Info (per serving): Calories: 450 | Fat: 25g | Carbs: 0g | Protein: 50g

Crispy Parmesan Chicken Tenders

Prep: 15 mins | Cook: 15 mins | Serves: 4

Ingredients:
- US: 500g chicken tenders, 60g grated Parmesan cheese, 60g breadcrumbs, 1 teaspoon garlic powder, 1 teaspoon dried parsley, salt, pepper, cooking spray
- UK: 500g chicken tenders, 60g grated Parmesan cheese, 60g breadcrumbs, 1 teaspoon garlic powder, 1 teaspoon dried parsley, salt, pepper, cooking spray

Instructions:
1. Preheat your air fryer toaster oven to 200°C (400°F).
2. In a shallow dish, mix together grated Parmesan cheese, breadcrumbs, garlic powder, dried parsley, salt, and pepper.
3. Dip each chicken tender into the breadcrumb mixture, pressing to coat evenly.
4. Place the coated chicken tenders in the air fryer basket in a single layer.
5. Lightly spray the chicken tenders with cooking spray.
6. Air fry for about 15 minutes, flipping halfway through, until chicken is golden brown and cooked through.
7. Once done, serve the Crispy Parmesan Chicken Tenders hot with your favorite dipping sauce.

Nutritional Info (per serving): Calories: 250 | Fat: 8g | Carbs: 10g | Protein: 35g

Cajun Spiced Pork Chops

Prep: 10 mins | Cook: 15 mins | Serves: 4

Ingredients:
- US: 4 pork chops (150g each), Cajun seasoning, salt, pepper, cooking spray
- UK: 4 pork chops (150g each), Cajun seasoning, salt, pepper, cooking spray

Instructions:
1. Preheat your air fryer toaster oven to 200°C (400°F).
2. Season both sides of the pork chops with Cajun seasoning, salt, and pepper.
3. Place the seasoned pork chops in the air fryer basket in a single layer.
4. Lightly spray the pork chops with cooking spray.
5. Air fry for about 15 minutes, flipping halfway through, until pork chops are cooked through.
6. Once done, let the pork chops rest for a few minutes before serving.
7. Serve the Cajun Spiced Pork Chops hot with your favorite sides.

Nutritional Info (per serving): Calories: 300 | Fat: 15g | Carbs: 0g | Protein: 40g

Honey Garlic Drumsticks

Prep: 10 mins | Cook: 25 mins | Serves: 4

Ingredients:
- US: 8 chicken drumsticks, 60ml honey, 30ml soy sauce, 2 cloves garlic (minced), 1 teaspoon grated ginger, salt, pepper, chopped green onions (for garnish)
- UK: 8 chicken drumsticks, 60ml honey, 30ml soy sauce, 2 cloves garlic (minced), 1 teaspoon grated ginger, salt, pepper, chopped green onions (for garnish)

Instructions:
1. Preheat your air fryer toaster oven to 180°C (350°F).
2. In a bowl, mix together honey, soy sauce, minced garlic, grated ginger, salt, and pepper.
3. Coat the chicken drumsticks with the honey garlic mixture.
4. Place the drumsticks in the air fryer basket in a single layer.
5. Air fry for about 25 minutes, flipping halfway through, until chicken is cooked through and golden brown.
6. Once done, sprinkle chopped green onions over the drumsticks before serving.
7. Serve the Honey Garlic Drumsticks hot with rice or vegetables.

Nutritional Info (per serving): Calories: 280 | Fat: 8g | Carbs: 20g | Protein: 30g

Meatballs with Marinara Sauce

Prep: 20 mins | Cook: 20 mins | Serves: 4

Ingredients:
- US: 500g ground beef, 1 egg, 60g breadcrumbs, 30g grated Parmesan cheese, 1 teaspoon dried oregano, 1 teaspoon dried basil, salt, pepper, 500ml marinara sauce, chopped fresh basil (for garnish)
- UK: 500g ground beef, 1 egg, 60g breadcrumbs, 30g grated Parmesan cheese, 1 teaspoon dried oregano, 1 teaspoon dried basil, salt, pepper, 500ml marinara sauce, chopped fresh basil (for garnish)

Instructions:
1. Preheat your air fryer toaster oven to 180°C (350°F).
2. In a bowl, mix together ground beef, egg, breadcrumbs, grated Parmesan cheese, dried oregano, dried basil, salt, and pepper until well combined.
3. Shape the mixture into meatballs.
4. Place the meatballs in the air fryer basket in a single layer.
5. Air fry for about 20 minutes, shaking the basket halfway through, until meatballs are cooked through and browned.
6. Once done, heat marinara sauce in a saucepan.
7. Serve the Meatballs with Marinara Sauce hot, garnished with chopped fresh basil.

Nutritional Info (per serving): Calories: 350 | Fat: 18g | Carbs: 15g | Protein: 30g

Philly Cheesesteak Stuffed Peppers

Prep: 15 mins | Cook: 20 mins | Serves: 4

Ingredients:
- US: 4 bell peppers (halved and seeds removed), 300g thinly sliced beef steak, 1 onion (sliced), 1 green bell pepper (sliced), 100g sliced mushrooms, 100g shredded provolone cheese, salt, pepper, cooking spray
- UK: 4 bell peppers (halved and seeds removed), 300g thinly sliced beef steak, 1 onion (sliced), 1 green bell pepper (sliced), 100g sliced mushrooms, 100g shredded provolone cheese, salt, pepper, cooking spray

Instructions:
1. Preheat your air fryer toaster oven to 180°C (350°F).
2. In a skillet, cook thinly sliced beef steak until browned.
3. Add sliced onion, green bell pepper, and mushrooms to the skillet and cook until softened.
4. Season the mixture with salt and pepper.
5. Fill each bell pepper half with the beef mixture.
6. Top each stuffed pepper with shredded provolone cheese.
7. Place the stuffed peppers in the air fryer basket in a single layer.
8. Lightly spray the stuffed peppers with cooking spray.

9. Air fry for about 20 minutes, until peppers are tender and cheese is melted and bubbly.
10. Once done, serve the Philly Cheesesteak Stuffed Peppers hot with a side salad.

Nutritional Info (per serving): Calories: 280 | Fat: 12g | Carbs: 15g | Protein: 30g

Air Fryer Turkey Burgers

Prep: 10 mins | Cook: 15 mins | Serves: 4

Ingredients:
- US: 500g ground turkey, 1 egg, 60g breadcrumbs, 1 teaspoon Worcestershire sauce, 1 teaspoon garlic powder, 1 teaspoon onion powder, salt, pepper, burger buns, lettuce, tomato slices, red onion slices
- UK: 500g ground turkey, 1 egg, 60g breadcrumbs, 1 teaspoon Worcestershire sauce, 1 teaspoon garlic powder, 1 teaspoon onion powder, salt, pepper, burger buns, lettuce, tomato slices, red onion slices

Instructions:
1. Preheat your air fryer toaster oven to 180°C (350°F).
2. In a bowl, mix together ground turkey, egg, breadcrumbs, Worcestershire sauce, garlic powder, onion powder, salt, and pepper until well combined.
3. Shape the mixture into burger patties.
4. Place the burger patties in the air fryer basket in a single layer.
5. Air fry for about 15 minutes, flipping halfway through, until burgers are cooked through and browned.
6. Once done, assemble the Air Fryer Turkey Burgers with lettuce, tomato slices, and red onion slices on burger buns.
7. Serve the turkey burgers hot with your favorite condiments.

Nutritional Info (per serving): Calories: 280 | Fat: 10g | Carbs: 25g | Protein: 20g

Coconut Lime Chicken Skewers

Prep: 20 mins | Cook: 15 mins | Serves: 4

Ingredients:
- US: 500g boneless, skinless chicken breasts (cut into cubes), 120ml coconut milk, 1 lime (juiced and zested), 2 cloves garlic (minced), 1 teaspoon ground ginger, 1 teaspoon curry powder, salt, pepper, cooking spray, lime wedges (for serving)
- UK: 500g boneless, skinless chicken breasts (cut into cubes), 120ml coconut milk, 1 lime (juiced and zested), 2 cloves garlic (minced), 1 teaspoon ground ginger, 1 teaspoon curry powder, salt, pepper, cooking spray, lime wedges (for serving)

Instructions:
1. Preheat your air fryer toaster oven to 180°C (350°F).
2. In a bowl, mix together coconut milk, lime juice and zest, minced garlic, ground ginger, curry powder, salt, and pepper.
3. Add chicken cubes to the marinade and toss to coat evenly.

4. Thread the marinated chicken onto skewers.
5. Lightly spray the chicken skewers with cooking spray.
6. Place the skewers in the air fryer basket in a single layer.
7. Air fry for about 15 minutes, turning halfway through, until chicken is cooked through and lightly browned.
8. Once done, serve the Coconut Lime Chicken Skewers hot with lime wedges for squeezing.

Nutritional Info (per serving): Calories: 250 | Fat: 10g | Carbs: 5g | Protein: 30g

Glazed Air Fryer Ham

Prep: 10 mins | Cook: 20 mins | Serves: 4

Ingredients:
- US: 500g cooked ham, 60ml maple syrup, 30ml Dijon mustard, 30ml apple cider vinegar, 15ml soy sauce, 1 teaspoon garlic powder, 1 teaspoon ground ginger, salt, pepper, pineapple slices (for serving)
- UK: 500g cooked ham, 60ml maple syrup, 30ml Dijon mustard, 30ml apple cider vinegar, 15ml soy sauce, 1 teaspoon garlic powder, 1 teaspoon ground ginger, salt, pepper, pineapple slices (for serving)

Instructions:
1. Preheat your air fryer toaster oven to 180°C (350°F).
2. In a bowl, whisk together maple syrup, Dijon mustard, apple cider vinegar, soy sauce, garlic powder, ground ginger, salt, and pepper to make the glaze.
3. Brush the glaze over the cooked ham, ensuring it's evenly coated.
4. Place the glazed ham in the air fryer basket.
5. Air fry for about 20 minutes, brushing with more glaze halfway through, until ham is heated through and caramelized.
6. Once done, let the ham rest for a few minutes before slicing.
7. Serve the Glazed Air Fryer Ham hot with pineapple slices.

Nutritional Info (per serving): Calories: 220 | Fat: 8g | Carbs: 15g | Protein: 20g

Greek Beef Kabobs

Prep: 20 mins | Cook: 15 mins | Serves: 4

Ingredients:
- US: 500g beef sirloin (cut into cubes), 1 red bell pepper (cut into chunks), 1 green bell pepper (cut into chunks), 1 red onion (cut into chunks), 120ml Greek yogurt, 1 lemon (juiced and zested), 2 cloves garlic (minced), 1 teaspoon dried oregano, salt, pepper, cooking spray
- UK: 500g beef sirloin (cut into cubes), 1 red bell pepper (cut into chunks), 1 green bell pepper (cut into chunks), 1 red onion (cut into chunks), 120ml Greek yogurt, 1 lemon (juiced and zested), 2 cloves garlic (minced), 1 teaspoon dried oregano, salt, pepper, cooking spray

Instructions:
1. Preheat your air fryer toaster oven to 180°C (350°F).

CHAPTER 6: PASTA, PIZZA & BREADS

Personal Deep Dish Pizzas
Prep: 15 mins | Cook: 20 mins | Serves: 2
Ingredients:
- US: 2 pizza dough balls, 200g each; 120ml pizza sauce; 120g shredded mozzarella cheese; 60g sliced pepperoni; 30g sliced black olives; 30g sliced mushrooms; olive oil for brushing
- UK: 2 pizza dough balls, 200g each; 120ml pizza sauce; 120g shredded mozzarella cheese; 60g sliced pepperoni; 30g sliced black olives; 30g sliced mushrooms; olive oil for brushing

Instructions:
1. Preheat air fryer toaster oven to 200°C.
2. Roll out pizza dough into two personalsized pizzas.
3. Spread pizza sauce evenly on each dough.
4. Top with mozzarella cheese, pepperoni, black olives, and mushrooms.
5. Brush edges of the crust with olive oil.
6. Cook pizzas in the air fryer for 1520 minutes until cheese is melted and crust is golden brown.
7. Serve hot and enjoy your personal deep dish pizzas!

Nutritional Info (per serving): Calories: 650 | Fat: 27g | Carbs: 72g | Protein: 30g

Garlic Knots
Prep: 10 mins | Cook: 12 mins | Serves: 4
Ingredients:
- US: 1 can (400g) refrigerated pizza dough; 60g butter, melted; 2 cloves garlic, minced; 15g grated Parmesan cheese; 1 tablespoon chopped fresh parsley
- UK: 1 can (400g) refrigerated pizza dough; 60g butter, melted; 2 cloves garlic, minced; 15g grated Parmesan cheese; 1 tablespoon chopped fresh parsley

Instructions:
1. Preheat air fryer toaster oven to 180°C.
2. Roll out pizza dough and cut into strips.
3. Tie each strip into a knot and place on the air fryer basket.
4. In a bowl, mix melted butter and minced garlic.
5. Brush garlic butter mixture over the knots.
6. Cook knots in the air fryer for 1012 minutes until golden brown.
7. Sprinkle with Parmesan cheese and chopped parsley before serving.
8. Serve warm and enjoy these delicious garlic knots!

Nutritional Info (per serving): Calories: 250 | Fat: 15g | Carbs: 25g | Protein: 5g

Baked Pasta Bites

Prep: 15 mins | Cook: 20 mins | Serves: 4

Ingredients:
- US: 200g pasta, cooked al dente; 240ml marinara sauce; 120g shredded mozzarella cheese; 30g grated Parmesan cheese; 1 teaspoon Italian seasoning; salt and pepper to taste; chopped fresh basil for garnish
- UK: 200g pasta, cooked al dente; 240ml marinara sauce; 120g shredded mozzarella cheese; 30g grated Parmesan cheese; 1 teaspoon Italian seasoning; salt and pepper to taste; chopped fresh basil for garnish

Instructions:
1. Preheat air fryer toaster oven to 180°C.
2. In a bowl, mix cooked pasta, marinara sauce, mozzarella cheese, Parmesan cheese, Italian seasoning, salt, and pepper.
3. Spoon pasta mixture into greased muffin cups.
4. Cook pasta bites in the air fryer for 1520 minutes until cheese is melted and bubbly.
5. Garnish with chopped fresh basil before serving.
6. Serve hot and enjoy these tasty baked pasta bites!

Nutritional Info (per serving): Calories: 300 | Fat: 10g | Carbs: 35g | Protein: 15g

Air Fryer Bagels

Prep: 15 mins | Cook: 15 mins | Serves: 4

Ingredients:
- US: 300g plain flour; 7g instant yeast; 1 teaspoon salt; 1 tablespoon sugar; 180ml warm water; 1 egg, beaten; sesame seeds or poppy seeds for topping
- UK: 300g plain flour; 7g instant yeast; 1 teaspoon salt; 1 tablespoon sugar; 180ml warm water; 1 egg, beaten; sesame seeds or poppy seeds for topping

Instructions:
1. In a bowl, mix flour, yeast, salt, and sugar.
2. Gradually add warm water and knead until a smooth dough forms.
3. Divide dough into 4 portions and shape into bagels.
4. Preheat air fryer toaster oven to 180°C.
5. Brush bagels with beaten egg and sprinkle with sesame seeds or poppy seeds.
6. Cook bagels in the air fryer for 1215 minutes until golden brown.
7. Allow to cool slightly before slicing and serving.
8. Enjoy your homemade air fryer bagels with your favorite toppings!

Nutritional Info (per serving): Calories: 250 | Fat: 2g | Carbs: 50g | Protein: 9g

Calzones

Prep: 20 mins | Cook: 15 mins | Serves: 4

Ingredients:
- US: 2 pizza dough balls, 200g each; 240ml marinara sauce; 120g shredded mozzarella cheese; 60g sliced pepperoni; 30g sliced black olives; 30g sliced mushrooms
- UK: 2 pizza dough balls, 200g each; 240ml marinara sauce; 120g shredded mozzarella cheese; 60g sliced pepperoni; 30g sliced black olives; 30g sliced mushrooms

Instructions:
1. Preheat air fryer toaster oven to 200°C.
2. Roll out pizza dough into two circles.
3. Spread marinara sauce on one half of each circle.
4. Top sauce with mozzarella cheese, pepperoni, black olives, and mushrooms.
5. Fold the other half of the dough over the toppings to form a halfmoon shape.
6. Press edges to seal and crimp with a fork.
7. Place calzones on the air fryer basket.
8. Cook calzones in the air fryer for 1215 minutes until golden brown.
9. Serve hot and enjoy these delicious handheld calzones!

Nutritional Info (per serving): Calories: 550 | Fat: 25g | Carbs: 60g | Protein: 20g

Chili Cheese Stuffed Pretzels

Prep: 20 mins | Cook: 15 mins | Serves: 4

Ingredients:
- US: 300g plain flour; 7g instant yeast; 1 teaspoon salt; 1 tablespoon sugar; 180ml warm water; 60g chili cheese spread; 30g shredded cheddar cheese; 1 egg, beaten; coarse salt for topping
- UK: 300g plain flour; 7g instant yeast; 1 teaspoon salt; 1 tablespoon sugar; 180ml warm water; 60g chili cheese spread; 30g shredded cheddar cheese; 1 egg, beaten; coarse salt for topping

Instructions:
1. In a bowl, mix flour, yeast, salt, and sugar.
2. Gradually add warm water and knead until a smooth dough forms.
3. Divide dough into 4 portions and roll each into a rope.
4. Flatten each rope and spread chili cheese spread and shredded cheddar cheese in the center.
5. Fold dough over the filling and seal edges.
6. Shape stuffed dough into pretzels.
7. Preheat air fryer toaster oven to 180°C.
8. Brush pretzels with beaten egg and sprinkle with coarse salt.
9. Cook pretzels in the air fryer for 1215 minutes until golden brown.

10. Serve warm and enjoy these flavorful chili cheese stuffed pretzels!

Nutritional Info (per serving): Calories: 350 | Fat: 10g | Carbs: 50g | Protein: 12g

Air Fryer Empanadas

Prep: 20 mins | Cook: 15 mins | Serves: 4

Ingredients:
- US: 2 sheets readymade pie crust; 240g ground beef; 1/2 onion, finely chopped; 1/2 bell pepper, finely chopped; 2 cloves garlic, minced; 1 teaspoon cumin; 1 teaspoon paprika; salt and pepper to taste; 1 egg, beaten
- UK: 2 sheets readymade pie crust; 240g ground beef; 1/2 onion, finely chopped; 1/2 bell pepper, finely chopped; 2 cloves garlic, minced; 1 teaspoon cumin; 1 teaspoon paprika; salt and pepper to taste; 1 egg, beaten

Instructions:
1. In a skillet, cook ground beef, onion, bell pepper, and garlic until beef is browned and vegetables are softened.
2. Add cumin, paprika, salt, and pepper. Stir well.
3. Roll out pie crust and cut into circles.
4. Spoon beef mixture onto each circle.
5. Fold dough over filling and crimp edges with a fork to seal.
6. Preheat air fryer toaster oven to 180°C.
7. Brush empanadas with beaten egg.
8. Cook empanadas in the air fryer for 1215 minutes until golden brown.
9. Serve hot and enjoy these savory air fryer empanadas!

Nutritional Info (per serving): Calories: 380 | Fat: 20g | Carbs: 30g | Protein: 18g

Toasted Ravioli Bites

Prep: 15 mins | Cook: 12 mins | Serves: 4

Ingredients:
- US: 200g cheese ravioli; 1 egg, beaten; 60g breadcrumbs; 30g grated Parmesan cheese; 1 teaspoon Italian seasoning; marinara sauce for dipping
- UK: 200g cheese ravioli; 1 egg, beaten; 60g breadcrumbs; 30g grated Parmesan cheese; 1 teaspoon Italian seasoning; marinara sauce for dipping

Instructions:
1. Cook ravioli according to package instructions until al dente.
2. Dip cooked ravioli in beaten egg, then coat with breadcrumbs mixed with Parmesan cheese and Italian seasoning.
3. Preheat air fryer toaster oven to 180°C.
4. Arrange coated ravioli in a single layer on the air fryer basket.
5. Cook ravioli in the air fryer for 1012 minutes until crispy and golden brown.
6. Serve hot with marinara sauce for dipping.

7. Enjoy these crunchy and delicious toasted ravioli bites!

Nutritional Info (per serving): Calories: 250 | Fat: 10g | Carbs: 30g | Protein: 10g

Cheesy Garlic Breadsticks

Prep: 10 mins | Cook: 12 mins | Serves: 4

Ingredients:
- US: 1 tube refrigerated breadstick dough; 60g butter, melted; 2 cloves garlic, minced; 30g grated Parmesan cheese; 1 teaspoon Italian seasoning; 120g shredded mozzarella cheese
- UK: 1 tube refrigerated breadstick dough; 60g butter, melted; 2 cloves garlic, minced; 30g grated Parmesan cheese; 1 teaspoon Italian seasoning; 120g shredded mozzarella cheese

Instructions:
1. Unroll breadstick dough and separate into sticks.
2. In a bowl, mix melted butter, minced garlic, Parmesan cheese, and Italian seasoning.
3. Brush butter mixture over breadsticks and sprinkle with shredded mozzarella cheese.
4. Preheat air fryer toaster oven to 180°C.
5. Arrange breadsticks on the air fryer basket.
6. Cook breadsticks in the air fryer for 10-12 minutes until golden brown and cheese is melted.
7. Serve warm and enjoy these cheesy garlic breadsticks!

Nutritional Info (per serving): Calories: 280 | Fat: 15g | Carbs: 30g | Protein: 8g

Stromboli

Prep: 20 mins | Cook: 15 mins | Serves: 4

Ingredients:
- US: 1 sheet readymade pizza dough; 120ml marinara sauce; 120g shredded mozzarella cheese; 60g sliced pepperoni; 30g sliced black olives; 30g sliced mushrooms; 1 egg, beaten
- UK: 1 sheet readymade pizza dough; 120ml marinara sauce; 120g shredded mozzarella cheese; 60g sliced pepperoni; 30g sliced black olives; 30g sliced mushrooms; 1 egg, beaten

Instructions:
1. Preheat air fryer toaster oven to 200°C.
2. Roll out pizza dough into a rectangle.
3. Spread marinara sauce over the dough, leaving a border around the edges.
4. Layer mozzarella cheese, pepperoni, black olives, and mushrooms on top of the sauce.
5. Roll up the dough tightly, starting from the long edge.
6. Place stromboli seam side down on the air fryer basket.
7. Brush stromboli with beaten egg.
8. Cook stromboli in the air fryer for 12-15 minutes until golden brown.
9. Allow to cool slightly before slicing and serving.
10. Enjoy your homemade stromboli, filled with delicious Italian flavors!

Nutritional Info (per serving): Calories: 450 | Fat: 20g | Carbs: 45g | Protein: 18g

CHAPTER 7: VEGETABLES & SIDES

Crispy Air Fryer Brussel Sprouts
Prep: 10 mins | Cook: 15 mins | Serves: 4
Ingredients:
- US: 500g Brussels sprouts (trimmed and halved), 30ml olive oil, 1 teaspoon garlic powder, 1 teaspoon paprika, salt, pepper
- UK: 500g Brussels sprouts (trimmed and halved), 30ml olive oil, 1 teaspoon garlic powder, 1 teaspoon paprika, salt, pepper

Instructions:
1. Preheat your air fryer toaster oven to 200°C (400°F).
2. In a bowl, toss Brussels sprouts with olive oil, garlic powder, paprika, salt, and pepper until well coated.
3. Spread the Brussels sprouts in the air fryer basket in a single layer.
4. Air fry for about 15 minutes, shaking the basket halfway through, until Brussels sprouts are crispy and browned.
5. Once done, serve the Crispy Air Fryer Brussels Sprouts hot as a delicious side dish.

Nutritional Info (per serving): Calories: 120 | Fat: 7g | Carbs: 12g | Protein: 5g

Parmesan Roasted Asparagus
Prep: 10 mins | Cook: 10 mins | Serves: 4
Ingredients:
- US: 500g asparagus spears, 30ml olive oil, 30g grated Parmesan cheese, 1 teaspoon garlic powder, salt, pepper
- UK: 500g asparagus spears, 30ml olive oil, 30g grated Parmesan cheese, 1 teaspoon garlic powder, salt, pepper

Instructions:
1. Preheat your air fryer toaster oven to 200°C (400°F).
2. Toss asparagus spears with olive oil, grated Parmesan cheese, garlic powder, salt, and pepper in a bowl until evenly coated.
3. Place the seasoned asparagus spears in the air fryer basket in a single layer.
4. Air fry for about 10 minutes, shaking the basket halfway through, until asparagus is tender and lightly browned.
5. Once done, serve the Parmesan Roasted Asparagus hot as a tasty side dish.

Nutritional Info (per serving): Calories: 90 | Fat: 7g | Carbs: 5g | Protein: 4g

Air Fryer Baked Potatoes

Prep: 5 mins | Cook: 40 mins | Serves: 4

Ingredients:
- US: 4 medium potatoes, 15ml olive oil, salt, pepper
- UK: 4 medium potatoes, 15ml olive oil, salt, pepper

Instructions:
1. Preheat your air fryer toaster oven to 200°C (400°F).
2. Pierce each potato several times with a fork.
3. Rub potatoes with olive oil and sprinkle with salt and pepper.
4. Place the potatoes in the air fryer basket.
5. Air fry for about 40 minutes, flipping halfway through, until potatoes are tender.
6. Once done, serve the Air Fryer Baked Potatoes hot with your favorite toppings.

Nutritional Info (per serving): Calories: 220 | Fat: 4g | Carbs: 45g | Protein: 5g

Garlic Parmesan Carrot Fries

Prep: 10 mins | Cook: 20 mins | Serves: 4

Ingredients:
- US: 500g carrots (peeled and cut into fries), 30ml olive oil, 30g grated Parmesan cheese, 2 cloves garlic (minced), 1 teaspoon dried parsley, salt, pepper
- UK: 500g carrots (peeled and cut into fries), 30ml olive oil, 30g grated Parmesan cheese, 2 cloves garlic (minced), 1 teaspoon dried parsley, salt, pepper

Instructions:
1. Preheat your air fryer toaster oven to 200°C (400°F).
2. In a bowl, toss carrot fries with olive oil, grated Parmesan cheese, minced garlic, dried parsley, salt, and pepper until well coated.
3. Spread the seasoned carrot fries in the air fryer basket in a single layer.
4. Air fry for about 20 minutes, shaking the basket halfway through, until carrot fries are crispy and golden brown.
5. Once done, serve the Garlic Parmesan Carrot Fries hot as a flavorful side dish.

Nutritional Info (per serving): Calories: 130 | Fat: 7g | Carbs: 15g | Protein: 3g

Hasselback Potatoes

Prep: 10 mins | Cook: 40 mins | Serves: 4

Ingredients:
- US: 4 medium potatoes, 60g butter (melted), 2 cloves garlic (minced), salt, pepper, chopped fresh parsley (for garnish)
- UK: 4 medium potatoes, 60g butter (melted), 2 cloves garlic (minced), salt, pepper, chopped fresh parsley (for garnish)

Instructions:
1. Preheat your air fryer toaster oven to 200°C (400°F).

2. Place a potato between two chopsticks or wooden spoons to prevent cutting all the way through.
3. Make thin slices across the potato, about 23mm apart, cutting almost to the bottom.
4. Mix melted butter and minced garlic in a bowl.
5. Brush the potatoes with the garlic butter mixture, making sure to get in between the slices.
6. Season the potatoes with salt and pepper.
7. Place the seasoned potatoes in the air fryer basket.
8. Air fry for about 40 minutes, until potatoes are crispy on the outside and tender on the inside.
9. Once done, garnish the Hasselback Potatoes with chopped fresh parsley before serving.

Nutritional Info (per serving): Calories: 250 | Fat: 12g | Carbs: 30g | Protein: 3g

Roasted Maple Dijon Carrots

Prep: 10 mins | Cook: 20 mins | Serves: 4

Ingredients:
- US: 500g carrots (peeled and sliced into sticks), 30ml olive oil, 30ml maple syrup, 15ml Dijon mustard, salt, pepper, chopped fresh parsley (for garnish)
- UK: 500g carrots (peeled and sliced into sticks), 30ml olive oil, 30ml maple syrup, 15ml Dijon mustard, salt, pepper, chopped fresh parsley (for garnish)

Instructions:
1. Preheat your air fryer toaster oven to 200°C (400°F).
2. In a bowl, whisk together olive oil, maple syrup, Dijon mustard, salt, and pepper.
3. Add carrot sticks to the bowl and toss until well coated.
4. Spread the coated carrots in the air fryer basket in a single layer.
5. Air fry for about 20 minutes, shaking the basket halfway through, until carrots are tender and caramelized.
6. Once done, garnish the Roasted Maple Dijon Carrots with chopped fresh parsley before serving.

Nutritional Info (per serving): Calories: 150 | Fat: 7g | Carbs: 20g | Protein: 1g

Crispy Smashed Potatoes

Prep: 10 mins | Cook: 30 mins | Serves: 4

Ingredients:
- US: 500g baby potatoes, 30ml olive oil, 2 cloves garlic (minced), salt, pepper, chopped fresh rosemary (for garnish)
- UK: 500g baby potatoes, 30ml olive oil, 2 cloves garlic (minced), salt, pepper, chopped fresh rosemary (for garnish)

Instructions:
1. Preheat your air fryer toaster oven to 200°C (400°F).
2. Boil the baby potatoes in salted water until tender, about 15 minutes.

3. Drain the potatoes and let them cool slightly.
4. Place the boiled potatoes on a baking sheet and gently smash them with a fork or potato masher.
5. Drizzle olive oil over the smashed potatoes and sprinkle with minced garlic, salt, and pepper.
6. Transfer the seasoned potatoes to the air fryer basket.
7. Air fry for about 30 minutes, until potatoes are crispy and golden brown.
8. Once done, garnish the Crispy Smashed Potatoes with chopped fresh rosemary before serving.

Nutritional Info (per serving): Calories: 180 | Fat: 7g | Carbs: 25g | Protein: 3g

Jalapeno Popper Stuffed Mushrooms

Prep: 15 mins | Cook: 15 mins | Serves: 4

Ingredients:
- US: 8 large mushrooms, 120g cream cheese, 60g shredded cheddar cheese, 2 jalapenos (seeded and finely diced), 2 cloves garlic (minced), salt, pepper, chopped fresh parsley (for garnish)
- UK: 8 large mushrooms, 120g cream cheese, 60g shredded cheddar cheese, 2 jalapenos (seeded and finely diced), 2 cloves garlic (minced), salt, pepper, chopped fresh parsley (for garnish)

Instructions:
1. Preheat your air fryer toaster oven to 180°C (350°F).
2. Remove the stems from the mushrooms and hollow out the caps slightly.
3. In a bowl, mix together cream cheese, shredded cheddar cheese, diced jalapenos, minced garlic, salt, and pepper until well combined.
4. Stuff each mushroom cap with the cheese mixture.
5. Place the stuffed mushrooms in the air fryer basket.
6. Air fry for about 15 minutes, until mushrooms are tender and filling is golden and bubbly.
7. Once done, garnish the Jalapeno Popper Stuffed Mushrooms with chopped fresh parsley before serving.

Nutritional Info (per serving): Calories: 120 | Fat: 10g | Carbs: 4g | Protein: 5g

Roasted Beet & Goat Cheese Salad

Prep: 15 mins | Cook: 30 mins | Serves: 4

Ingredients:
- US: 500g beets (peeled and cut into cubes), 30ml olive oil, salt, pepper, 100g goat cheese, 50g walnuts (chopped), mixed salad greens
- UK: 500g beets (peeled and cut into cubes), 30ml olive oil, salt, pepper, 100g goat cheese, 50g walnuts (chopped), mixed salad greens

Instructions:
1. Preheat your air fryer toaster oven to 200°C (400°F).

2. In a bowl, mix together Greek yogurt, lemon juice and zest, minced garlic, dried oregano, salt, and pepper to make the marinade.
3. Add beef cubes to the marinade and toss to coat evenly.
4. Thread marinated beef, bell peppers, and onion onto skewers.
5. Lightly spray the kabobs with cooking spray.
6. Place the kabobs in the air fryer basket in a single layer.
7. Air fry for about 15 minutes, turning halfway through, until beef is cooked to desired doneness and vegetables are tender.
8. Once done, serve the Greek Beef Kabobs hot with rice or pita bread.

Nutritional Info (per serving): Calories: 300 | Fat: 12g | Carbs: 10g | Protein: 40g

CHAPTER 5: SEAFOOD

Coconut Shrimp with Pineapple Salsa
Prep: 15 mins | Cook: 10 mins | Serves: 4
Ingredients:
- US: 500g large shrimp (peeled and deveined), 100g shredded coconut, 60g breadcrumbs, 2 eggs (beaten), salt, pepper, cooking spray
- UK: 500g large prawns (peeled and deveined), 100g desiccated coconut, 60g breadcrumbs, 2 eggs (beaten), salt, pepper, cooking spray

Instructions:
1. Preheat your air fryer to 200°C (400°F).
2. In one bowl, mix shredded coconut and breadcrumbs. In another bowl, beat eggs with salt and pepper.
3. Dip each shrimp in the egg mixture, then coat with the coconut breadcrumb mixture.
4. Place the coated shrimp in the air fryer basket in a single layer.
5. Lightly spray the shrimp with cooking spray.
6. Air fry for 810 minutes until golden brown and crispy.
7. Serve with pineapple salsa on the side.

Nutritional Info: Calories: 280 | Fat: 12g | Carbs: 18g | Protein: 24g

Lemon Dill Salmon Patties
Prep: 15 mins | Cook: 10 mins | Serves: 4
Ingredients:
- US: 400g canned salmon, 1 egg, 30g breadcrumbs, 1 tablespoon lemon juice, 1 tablespoon chopped fresh dill, salt, pepper, olive oil (for brushing)
- UK: 400g canned salmon, 1 egg, 30g breadcrumbs, 1 tablespoon lemon juice, 1 tablespoon chopped fresh dill, salt, pepper, olive oil (for brushing)

Instructions:
1. Drain the canned salmon and remove any bones.
2. In a bowl, mix together salmon, egg, breadcrumbs, lemon juice, dill, salt, and pepper.
3. Form the mixture into patties.
4. Preheat the air fryer to 180°C (350°F).
5. Brush each patty with olive oil on both sides.
6. Place the patties in the air fryer basket.
7. Air fry for 810 minutes, flipping halfway through, until golden brown and cooked through.
8. Serve hot with a squeeze of lemon.

Nutritional Info: Calories: 220 | Fat: 10g | Carbs: 8g | Protein: 24g

Crispy Fried Fish Sandwiches
Prep: 15 mins | Cook: 15 mins | Serves: 4
Ingredients:
- US: 4 white fish fillets (such as cod or haddock), 100g flour, 2 eggs (beaten), 100g breadcrumbs, salt, pepper, cooking spray, 4 burger buns, lettuce, tomato slices, tartar sauce
- UK: 4 white fish fillets (such as cod or haddock), 100g plain flour, 2 eggs (beaten), 100g breadcrumbs, salt, pepper, cooking spray, 4 burger buns, lettuce, tomato slices, tartar sauce

Instructions:
1. Season fish fillets with salt and pepper.
2. Set up a breading station: one bowl of flour, one bowl of beaten eggs, and one bowl of breadcrumbs.
3. Dredge each fish fillet in flour, then dip in egg, and coat with breadcrumbs.
4. Preheat the air fryer to 200°C (400°F).
5. Spray the air fryer basket with cooking spray.
6. Place the breaded fish fillets in the basket.
7. Air fry for 1215 minutes until crispy and cooked through.
8. Toast burger buns in the air fryer if desired.
9. Assemble sandwiches with lettuce, tomato, fish fillet, and tartar sauce.

Nutritional Info: Calories: 350 | Fat: 10g | Carbs: 38g | Protein: 26g

Cajun Air Fryer Shrimp
Prep: 10 mins | Cook: 8 mins | Serves: 4
Ingredients:
- US: 500g large shrimp (peeled and deveined), 30ml olive oil, 1 tablespoon Cajun seasoning, 1 teaspoon garlic powder, 1 teaspoon paprika, salt, lemon wedges (for serving)
- UK: 500g large prawns (peeled and deveined), 30ml olive oil, 1 tablespoon Cajun seasoning, 1 teaspoon garlic powder, 1 teaspoon paprika, salt, lemon wedges (for serving)

Instructions:
1. In a bowl, toss shrimp with olive oil, Cajun seasoning, garlic powder, paprika, and salt.
2. Preheat the air fryer to 200°C (400°F).
3. Spread the seasoned shrimp in the air fryer basket in a single layer.
4. Air fry for 68 minutes until shrimp are pink and cooked through.
5. Serve hot with lemon wedges for squeezing.

Nutritional Info: Calories: 180 | Fat: 8g | Carbs: 2g | Protein: 24g

Pesto Crusted Salmon Fillets

Prep: 10 mins | Cook: 12 mins | Serves: 4

Ingredients:
- US: 4 salmon fillets, 60g pesto sauce, 30g breadcrumbs, lemon wedges (for serving)
- UK: 4 salmon fillets, 60g pesto sauce, 30g breadcrumbs, lemon wedges (for serving)

Instructions:
1. Spread pesto sauce evenly over each salmon fillet.
2. Sprinkle breadcrumbs over the pesto layer, pressing lightly to adhere.
3. Preheat the air fryer to 180°C (350°F).
4. Place the salmon fillets in the air fryer basket.
5. Air fry for 10-12 minutes until salmon is cooked through and topping is golden brown.
6. Serve hot with lemon wedges on the side.

Nutritional Info: Calories: 280 | Fat: 15g | Carbs: 5g | Protein: 30g

Tuna Poke Bowl

Prep: 20 mins | Cook: 0 mins | Serves: 2

Ingredients:
- US: 200g sushi-grade tuna (cubed), 1 avocado (sliced), 1 cup cooked sushi rice, 1/4 cup soy sauce, 1 tablespoon sesame oil, 1 tablespoon rice vinegar, 1 tablespoon sesame seeds, sliced cucumber, sliced radishes, sliced green onions
- UK: 200g sushi-grade tuna (cubed), 1 avocado (sliced), 1 cup cooked sushi rice, 1/4 cup soy sauce, 1 tablespoon sesame oil, 1 tablespoon rice vinegar, 1 tablespoon sesame seeds, sliced cucumber, sliced radishes, sliced spring onions

Instructions:
1. In a bowl, mix together soy sauce, sesame oil, rice vinegar, and sesame seeds to make the marinade.
2. Add cubed tuna to the marinade and let it sit for 10 minutes.
3. Divide cooked rice between two bowls.
4. Top with marinated tuna, sliced avocado, cucumber, radishes, and green onions.
5. Drizzle with extra marinade if desired.
6. Serve immediately as a refreshing seafood bowl.

Nutritional Info: Calories: 400 | Fat: 20g | Carbs: 35g | Protein: 25g

Asian Glazed Cod

Prep: 10 mins | Cook: 10 mins | Serves: 4

Ingredients:
- US: 4 cod fillets, 60ml soy sauce, 30ml honey, 2 cloves garlic (minced), 1 teaspoon grated ginger, 1 tablespoon sesame oil, sliced green onions (for garnish)
- UK: 4 cod fillets, 60ml soy sauce, 30ml honey, 2 cloves garlic (minced), 1 teaspoon grated ginger, 1 tablespoon sesame oil, sliced spring onions (for garnish)

Instructions:
1. In a bowl, whisk together soy sauce, honey, garlic, ginger, and sesame oil to make the glaze.
2. Place cod fillets in a shallow dish and pour the glaze over them. Let them marinate for 10 minutes.
3. Preheat the air fryer to 180°C (350°F).
4. Place marinated cod fillets in the air fryer basket.
5. Air fry for 8-10 minutes until fish flakes easily with a fork.
6. Garnish with sliced green onions before serving.

Nutritional Info: Calories: 220 | Fat: 5g | Carbs: 15g | Protein: 25g

Shrimp Fajitas

Prep: 15 mins | Cook: 10 mins | Serves: 4

Ingredients:
- US: 500g shrimp (peeled and deveined), 2 bell peppers (sliced), 1 onion (sliced), 2 tablespoons fajita seasoning, 2 tablespoons olive oil, tortillas, sour cream, salsa, guacamole (for serving)
- UK: 500g prawns (peeled and deveined), 2 bell peppers (sliced), 1 onion (sliced), 2 tablespoons fajita seasoning, 2 tablespoons olive oil, tortillas, sour cream, salsa, guacamole (for serving)

Instructions:
1. In a bowl, toss shrimp, sliced bell peppers, onion, fajita seasoning, and olive oil until well coated.
2. Preheat the air fryer to 200°C (400°F).
3. Spread the seasoned shrimp and vegetables in the air fryer basket.
4. Air fry for 8-10 minutes, shaking the basket halfway through, until shrimp are pink and vegetables are tender.
5. Serve shrimp and vegetables with tortillas and your favorite toppings.

Nutritional Info: Calories: 320 | Fat: 10g | Carbs: 35g | Protein: 25g

Crab Cake Sliders

Prep: 20 mins | Cook: 10 mins | Serves: 4

Ingredients:
- US: 200g lump crabmeat, 1 egg, 30g breadcrumbs, 1 tablespoon mayonnaise, 1 teaspoon Dijon mustard, 1/2 teaspoon Worcestershire sauce, salt, pepper, slider buns, lettuce, tomato slices, tartar sauce
- UK: 200g lump crabmeat, 1 egg, 30g breadcrumbs, 1 tablespoon mayonnaise, 1 teaspoon Dijon mustard, 1/2 teaspoon Worcestershire sauce, salt, pepper, slider buns, lettuce, tomato slices, tartar sauce

Instructions:
1. In a bowl, mix together crabmeat, egg, breadcrumbs, mayonnaise, mustard, Worcestershire sauce, salt, and pepper.
2. Form the mixture into small patties.
3. Preheat the air fryer to 180°C (350°F).
4. Place the crab cake sliders in the air fryer basket.
5. Air fry for 8-10 minutes until golden brown and cooked through.
6. Serve on slider buns with lettuce, tomato, and tartar sauce.

Nutritional Info: Calories: 220 | Fat: 8g | Carbs: 20g | Protein: 15g

Crispy Calamari

Prep: 20 mins | Cook: 10 mins | Serves: 4

Ingredients:
- US: 300g calamari rings, 100g flour, 2 eggs (beaten), 100g breadcrumbs, salt, pepper, lemon wedges (for serving), marinara sauce (for dipping)
- UK: 300g squid rings, 100g plain flour, 2 eggs (beaten), 100g breadcrumbs, salt, pepper, lemon wedges (for serving), marinara sauce (for dipping)

Instructions:
1. Pat calamari rings dry with paper towels.
2. Set up a breading station: one bowl of flour, one bowl of beaten eggs, and one bowl of breadcrumbs seasoned with salt and pepper.
3. Dredge each calamari ring in flour, then dip in egg, and coat with breadcrumbs.
4. Preheat the air fryer to 200°C (400°F).
5. Place the breaded calamari rings in the air fryer basket in a single layer.
6. Air fry for 8-10 minutes until golden brown and crispy.
7. Serve hot with lemon wedges and marinara sauce for dipping.

Nutritional Info: Calories: 280 | Fat: 10g | Carbs: 30g | Protein: 20g

2. Toss beet cubes with olive oil, salt, and pepper in a bowl until evenly coated.
3. Spread the seasoned beets in the air fryer basket in a single layer.
4. Air fry for about 30 minutes, shaking the basket halfway through, until beets are tender and caramelized.
5. Once done, let the roasted beets cool slightly.
6. In a large bowl, combine roasted beets, mixed salad greens, crumbled goat cheese, and chopped walnuts.
7. Toss the salad gently to combine.
8. Serve the Roasted Beet & Goat Cheese Salad as a delightful side or light meal.

Nutritional Info (per serving): Calories: 250 | Fat: 15g | Carbs: 20g | Protein: 10g

Honey Roasted Parsnip Fries

Prep: 10 mins | Cook: 25 mins | Serves: 4

Ingredients:
- US: 500g parsnips (peeled and cut into fries), 30ml olive oil, 30ml honey, 1 teaspoon ground cumin, salt, pepper
- UK: 500g parsnips (peeled and cut into fries), 30ml olive oil, 30ml honey, 1 teaspoon ground cumin, salt, pepper

Instructions:
1. Preheat your air fryer toaster oven to 200°C (400°F).
2. In a bowl, mix together olive oil, honey, ground cumin, salt, and pepper.
3. Add parsnip fries to the bowl and toss until well coated.
4. Spread the coated parsnip fries in the air fryer basket in a single layer.
5. Air fry for about 25 minutes, shaking the basket halfway through, until parsnip fries are crispy and golden brown.
6. Once done, serve the Honey Roasted Parsnip Fries hot as a tasty side dish.

Nutritional Info (per serving): Calories: 180 | Fat: 7g | Carbs: 30g | Protein: 2g

CHAPTER 8: COMFORT FOODS

Air Fryer Chicken Pot Pie
Prep: 20 mins | Cook: 25 mins | Serves: 4
Ingredients:
- US: 2 cooked chicken breasts (diced), 1 cup frozen mixed vegetables, 1/2 cup chicken broth, 2 tablespoons allpurpose flour, 1/4 cup milk, salt, pepper, 1 refrigerated pie crust
- UK: 2 cooked chicken breasts (diced), 150g frozen mixed vegetables, 120ml chicken broth, 2 tablespoons plain flour, 60ml milk, salt, pepper, 1 refrigerated shortcrust pastry

Instructions:
1. In a saucepan, combine chicken, mixed vegetables, chicken broth, flour, milk, salt, and pepper.
2. Cook over medium heat until thickened, stirring constantly.
3. Preheat the air fryer to 180°C (350°F).
4. Pour the chicken mixture into individual ramekins.
5. Roll out the pie crust and cut into circles to fit the ramekins.
6. Place the pie crust over each ramekin, sealing the edges.
7. Cut a few slits in the crust to vent.
8. Air fry for 2025 minutes until the crust is golden brown and the filling is bubbly.
9. Let cool for a few minutes before serving.

Nutritional Info: Calories: 350 | Fat: 15g | Carbs: 30g | Protein: 20g

Mini Deep Dish Chicken Pot Pies
Prep: 20 mins | Cook: 25 mins | Serves: 4
Ingredients:
- US: 2 cooked chicken breasts (diced), 1 cup frozen mixed vegetables, 1/2 cup chicken broth, 2 tablespoons allpurpose flour, 1/4 cup milk, salt, pepper, 1 refrigerated pie crust
- UK: 2 cooked chicken breasts (diced), 150g frozen mixed vegetables, 120ml chicken broth, 2 tablespoons plain flour, 60ml milk, salt, pepper, 1 refrigerated shortcrust pastry

Instructions:
1. In a saucepan, combine chicken, mixed vegetables, chicken broth, flour, milk, salt, and pepper.
2. Cook over medium heat until thickened, stirring constantly.
3. Preheat the air fryer to 180°C (350°F).
4. Roll out the pie crust and cut into circles to fit a muffin tin.
5. Press the pie crust circles into greased muffin cups, forming mini pie crusts.
6. Divide the chicken mixture among the mini pie crusts.
7. Roll out remaining pie crust and cut small circles to cover each mini pie.
8. Seal the edges and cut slits in the top crusts for venting.
9. Air fry for 2025 minutes until the crust is golden brown and the filling is bubbly.

10. Let cool for a few minutes before serving.

Nutritional Info: Calories: 300 | Fat: 12g | Carbs: 25g | Protein: 18g

Shepherd's Pie

Prep: 30 mins | Cook: 30 mins | Serves: 4

Ingredients:
- US: 500g ground beef, 1 onion (chopped), 2 carrots (diced), 1 cup frozen peas, 2 tablespoons tomato paste, 1 cup beef broth, 2 cups mashed potatoes, salt, pepper, 50g grated cheddar cheese
- UK: 500g minced beef, 1 onion (chopped), 2 carrots (diced), 150g frozen peas, 2 tablespoons tomato paste, 240ml beef broth, 400g mashed potatoes, salt, pepper, 50g grated cheddar cheese

Instructions:
1. In a skillet, cook ground beef and onion until browned.
2. Add carrots, peas, tomato paste, and beef broth. Simmer for 10 minutes.
3. Season with salt and pepper to taste.
4. Preheat the air fryer to 180°C (350°F).
5. Transfer the beef mixture to a baking dish.
6. Spread mashed potatoes over the beef mixture.
7. Sprinkle grated cheddar cheese on top.
8. Air fry for 25-30 minutes until the cheese is melted and bubbly.
9. Let cool for a few minutes before serving.

Nutritional Info: Calories: 400 | Fat: 20g | Carbs: 30g | Protein: 25g

Air Fryer Pigs in a Blanket

Prep: 10 mins | Cook: 10 mins | Serves: 4

Ingredients:
- US: 8 cocktail sausages, 1 sheet puff pastry, mustard (for serving)
- UK: 8 cocktail sausages, 1 sheet puff pastry, mustard (for serving)

Instructions:
1. Cut puff pastry into strips.
2. Wrap each cocktail sausage with a strip of puff pastry.
3. Preheat the air fryer to 180°C (350°F).
4. Place pigs in a blanket in the air fryer basket.
5. Air fry for 8-10 minutes until golden brown and puffed.
6. Serve hot with mustard for dipping.

Nutritional Info: Calories: 220 | Fat: 15g | Carbs: 15g | Protein: 8g

Chicken & Dumplings

Prep: 20 mins | Cook: 25 mins | Serves: 4

Ingredients:
- US: 2 cooked chicken breasts (shredded), 1 onion (chopped), 2 carrots (diced), 2 celery stalks (chopped), 1 cup frozen peas, 4 cups chicken broth, 1 cup milk, 1 cup allpurpose flour, 2 teaspoons baking powder, 1/2 teaspoon salt, 1/2 cup chopped fresh parsley
- UK: 2 cooked chicken breasts (shredded), 1 onion (chopped), 2 carrots (diced), 2 celery stalks (chopped), 150g frozen peas, 960ml chicken broth, 240ml milk, 120g plain flour, 10g baking powder, 1/2 teaspoon salt, 15g chopped fresh parsley

Instructions:
1. In a pot, combine chicken, onion, carrots, celery, peas, and chicken broth. Bring to a boil.
2. In a bowl, mix flour, baking powder, and salt. Stir in milk to form a dough.
3. Drop spoonfuls of dough into the boiling broth mixture.
4. Cover and simmer for 15 minutes.
5. Preheat the air fryer to 180°C (350°F).
6. Transfer the chicken and dumplings to a baking dish.
7. Air fry for 1015 minutes until the top is golden brown.
8. Garnish with chopped parsley before serving.

Nutritional Info: Calories: 350 | Fat: 10g | Carbs: 40g | Protein: 25g

Beef & Cheddar Hand Pies

Prep: 20 mins | Cook: 25 mins | Serves: 4

Ingredients:
- US: 300g ground beef, 1 onion (chopped), 1 teaspoon Worcestershire sauce, salt, pepper, 1 sheet puff pastry, 100g grated cheddar cheese, 1 egg (beaten)
- UK: 300g minced beef, 1 onion (chopped), 1 teaspoon Worcestershire sauce, salt, pepper, 1 sheet puff pastry, 100g grated cheddar cheese, 1 egg (beaten)

Instructions:
1. In a skillet, cook ground beef and onion until browned.
2. Season with Worcestershire sauce, salt, and pepper.
3. Preheat the air fryer to 180°C (350°F).
4. Roll out puff pastry and cut into squares.
5. Place a spoonful of beef mixture and grated cheddar cheese onto each square.
6. Fold pastry over to form a triangle and crimp edges with a fork.
7. Brush hand pies with beaten egg.
8. Air fry for 2025 minutes until golden brown and crispy.
9. Let cool for a few minutes before serving.

Nutritional Info: Calories: 380 | Fat: 25g | Carbs: 25g | Protein: 20g

Mac & Cheese Bites
Prep: 15 mins | Cook: 10 mins | Serves: 4
Ingredients:
- US: 200g macaroni, 1 cup shredded cheddar cheese, 1/4 cup milk, 1 egg (beaten), 1/2 cup breadcrumbs, salt, pepper
- UK: 200g macaroni, 100g grated cheddar cheese, 60ml milk, 1 egg (beaten), 50g breadcrumbs, salt, pepper

Instructions:
1. Cook macaroni according to package instructions. Drain.
2. In a bowl, mix cooked macaroni, cheddar cheese, milk, beaten egg, salt, and pepper.
3. Preheat the air fryer to 200°C (400°F).
4. Shape the mac and cheese mixture into balls.
5. Roll each ball in breadcrumbs to coat.
6. Place the mac and cheese bites in the air fryer basket.
7. Air fry for 810 minutes until golden and crispy.
8. Serve hot as a tasty snack or side dish.

Nutritional Info: Calories: 280 | Fat: 12g | Carbs: 30g | Protein: 15g

Air Fryer Monte Cristo Sandwiches
Prep: 10 mins | Cook: 10 mins | Serves: 2
Ingredients:
- US: 4 slices bread, 4 slices ham, 4 slices turkey, 4 slices Swiss cheese, 2 eggs (beaten), 1/4 cup milk, salt, pepper, powdered sugar (for dusting), raspberry jam (for dipping)
- UK: 4 slices bread, 4 slices ham, 4 slices turkey, 4 slices Swiss cheese, 2 eggs (beaten), 60ml milk, salt, pepper, powdered sugar (for dusting), raspberry jam (for dipping)

Instructions:
1. Assemble sandwiches with ham, turkey, and Swiss cheese between bread slices.
2. In a shallow dish, whisk together beaten eggs, milk, salt, and pepper.
3. Dip each sandwich into the egg mixture, coating both sides.
4. Preheat the air fryer to 180°C (350°F).
5. Place sandwiches in the air fryer basket.
6. Air fry for 45 minutes per side until golden brown and cheese is melted.
7. Dust with powdered sugar before serving.
8. Serve with raspberry jam for dipping.

Nutritional Info: Calories: 450 | Fat: 20g | Carbs: 35g | Protein: 30g

Buffalo Chicken Egg Rolls

Prep: 20 mins | Cook: 10 mins | Serves: 4

Ingredients:
- US: 2 cups shredded cooked chicken, 1/2 cup buffalo sauce, 1/2 cup shredded mozzarella cheese, 8 egg roll wrappers, oil for frying, ranch dressing (for dipping)
- UK: 240g shredded cooked chicken, 120ml buffalo sauce, 60g shredded mozzarella cheese, 8 egg roll wrappers, oil for frying, ranch dressing (for dipping)

Instructions:
1. In a bowl, mix shredded chicken and buffalo sauce.
2. Stir in shredded mozzarella cheese.
3. Place a spoonful of chicken mixture onto each egg roll wrapper.
4. Roll up, tucking in sides, and seal edges with water.
5. Preheat the air fryer to 200°C (400°F).
6. Brush egg rolls with oil.
7. Air fry for 810 minutes until golden and crispy.
8. Serve hot with ranch dressing for dipping.

Nutritional Info: Calories: 320 | Fat: 15g | Carbs: 25g | Protein: 20g

Crispy Chicken Parmesan

Prep: 15 mins | Cook: 15 mins | Serves: 4

Ingredients:
- US: 4 boneless, skinless chicken breasts, 1 cup breadcrumbs, 1/2 cup grated Parmesan cheese, 1 teaspoon Italian seasoning, salt, pepper, 1 egg (beaten), marinara sauce, shredded mozzarella cheese, cooked spaghetti (for serving)
- UK: 4 boneless, skinless chicken breasts, 100g breadcrumbs, 50g grated Parmesan cheese, 1 teaspoon Italian seasoning, salt, pepper, 1 egg (beaten), marinara sauce, shredded mozzarella cheese, cooked spaghetti (for serving)

Instructions:
1. In a shallow dish, mix breadcrumbs, Parmesan cheese, Italian seasoning, salt, and pepper.
2. Dip each chicken breast in beaten egg, then coat with breadcrumb mixture.
3. Preheat the air fryer to 200°C (400°F).
4. Place breaded chicken breasts in the air fryer basket.
5. Air fry for 1215 minutes until chicken is golden and cooked through.
6. Spoon marinara sauce over each chicken breast.
7. Top with shredded mozzarella cheese.
8. Air fry for an additional 23 minutes until cheese is melted and bubbly.
9. Serve hot with cooked spaghetti.

Nutritional Info: Calories: 350 | Fat: 15g | Carbs: 20g | Protein: 30g

Holiday Wreath Bread

Prep: 20 mins | Cook: 30 mins | Serves: 8

Ingredients:
- US: 500g pizza dough, 60g butter (melted), 2 cloves garlic (minced), 1 teaspoon dried oregano, 60g grated Parmesan cheese, marinara sauce (for serving)
- UK: 500g pizza dough, 60g butter (melted), 2 cloves garlic (minced), 1 teaspoon dried oregano, 60g grated Parmesan cheese, marinara sauce (for serving)

Instructions:
1. Preheat your air fryer toaster oven to 180°C (350°F).
2. Roll out the pizza dough into a large circle on a lightly floured surface.
3. Using a sharp knife or pizza cutter, make cuts around the edge of the dough, leaving the center intact to resemble a wreath.
4. In a bowl, mix together melted butter, minced garlic, dried oregano, and grated Parmesan cheese.
5. Brush the garlic parmesan butter mixture over the dough, including the cut edges.
6. Transfer the prepared dough to a baking sheet lined with parchment paper.
7. Bake in the preheated oven for about 2530 minutes, until the bread is golden brown and cooked through.
8. Once done, serve the Holiday Wreath Bread warm with marinara sauce for dipping.

Nutritional Info (per serving): Calories: 280 | Fat: 12g | Carbs: 35g | Protein: 8g

Fried Ravioli Skewers

Prep: 20 mins | Cook: 15 mins | Serves: 4

Ingredients:
- US: 250g fresh ravioli (any flavor), 2 eggs (beaten), breadcrumbs, marinara sauce (for serving)
- UK: 250g fresh ravioli (any flavor), 2 eggs (beaten), breadcrumbs, marinara sauce (for serving)

Instructions:
1. Preheat your air fryer toaster oven to 200°C (400°F).
2. Dip each ravioli in beaten egg, then coat with breadcrumbs.
3. Thread the coated ravioli onto skewers.
4. Place the ravioli skewers in the air fryer basket.
5. Air fry for about 15 minutes, until the ravioli is golden brown and crispy.
6. Once done, serve the Fried Ravioli Skewers hot with marinara sauce for dipping.

Nutritional Info (per serving): Calories: 220 | Fat: 10g | Carbs: 25g | Protein: 8g

CONCLUSION

As you flip through the delicious recipes and helpful insights in this comprehensive cookbook, I hope you feel inspired to tap into the full potential of your air fryer toaster oven. This remarkable appliance truly is a culinary game changer that will transform how you cook at home.

With the air fryer function, you'll be able to enjoy crispy fried favorites like chicken wings, fries, and empanadas with a mere fraction of the fat and calories. The rapid air circulation creates that signature crunchy texture using little to no oil at all. Gone are the days of dealing with splattering grease, lingering smells, and loads of dishwashing after frying.

Beyond frying, your air fryer toaster oven also serves as a compact oven for baking, roasting, broiling, dehydrating and more. In these pages, you'll find entire chapters filled with recipes for crispy baked goods, roasted meats and veggies, bubbling baked pastas, handheld pies and pockets, dehydrated healthy snacks, and even decadent desserts all tailored specifically for the air fryer oven.

Making a wholesome, indulgent meal has never been faster or easier. Simply toss your ingredients with a light mist of oil, spread in the cooking tray or fryer basket, set the temp and function, and walk away. Most recipes are ready in under 30 minutes with little hands on effort from you.

As you start experimenting with air fryer cooking, you'll be amazed at the juicy, evenly cooked results on the inside with the perfectly crisp, golden brown exterior. Every bite will have maximum flavor and crunch using a fraction of the oil, fat and calories compared to traditional frying or oven cooking.

Along with delicious recipes, you've also gained valuable knowledge on how to properly select, use, and care for your air fryer toaster oven. This book provides a deep grounding in how the appliance works, accessories to consider, adjustments for converting recipes, and time/temp guidance to ensure success.

With helpful labels, nutrition stats, meal prep plans and shopping lists, you can easily customize your air fryer cooking to suit any dietary needs or schedules. Spend less time planning and prepping, and more time enjoying the crispy, crave able results.

Of course, no culinary experience is complete without the occasional indulgence. The decadent dessert chapter lets you have your cake, cookies, and crispy treats while staying on the healthier side. Recipes like baked apples, lava cakes, and churros with air fryer ease deliver warmly spiced, molten, and golden crisp rewards.

I truly hope this book becomes a go to resource that expands your culinary horizons, streamlines your cooking routine, and enables you to eat healthier without sacrifice. Create fast, fresh family meals in a fraction of the time. Rediscover your favorite fried indulgences in a lighter way. Or explore creative, air fryer spins on classics. With this invaluable guide, the possibilities are endless. Most of all, I hope the recipes in these pages bring you tremendous satisfaction, joy, and connection through the act of cooking and sharing good food with loved ones. Cooking nourishes the body, mind, and soul. Now you can nourish yourself with maximum flavor and ease thanks to your air fryer toaster oven.

No matter warty road life takes you down, I encourage you to keep coming back to this cookbook as a source of inspiration in the kitchen. May every crispy, golden-brown bite bring you comfort and delight for years to come. **Happy air frying!**

Printed in Great Britain
by Amazon

CHAPTER 9: DESSERTS

Air Fryer Donuts

Prep: 15 mins | Cook: 10 mins | Serves: 6

Ingredients:
- US: 250g allpurpose flour; 50g granulated sugar; 1 teaspoon baking powder; 1/4 teaspoon salt; 120ml milk; 1 egg, beaten; 30g butter, melted; 1 teaspoon vanilla extract; oil spray
- UK: 250g allpurpose flour; 50g granulated sugar; 1 teaspoon baking powder; 1/4 teaspoon salt; 120ml milk; 1 egg, beaten; 30g butter, melted; 1 teaspoon vanilla extract; oil spray

Instructions:
1. In a bowl, mix flour, sugar, baking powder, and salt.
2. Stir in milk, beaten egg, melted butter, and vanilla extract until a dough forms.
3. Roll out dough and cut into donut shapes using a cutter.
4. Preheat air fryer toaster oven to 180°C.
5. Spray donuts with oil spray and place in the air fryer basket.
6. Cook donuts in the air fryer for 5 minutes, then flip and cook for another 5 minutes until golden brown.
7. Remove from air fryer and let cool slightly before serving.
8. Enjoy your homemade air fryer donuts with your favorite toppings!

Nutritional Info (per serving): Calories: 200 | Fat: 5g | Carbs: 35g | Protein: 5g

Baked Apples with Granola Topping

Prep: 10 mins | Cook: 20 mins | Serves: 4

Ingredients:
- US: 4 apples, cored and halved; 60g granola; 30g brown sugar; 30g butter, melted; 1 teaspoon cinnamon
- UK: 4 apples, cored and halved; 60g granola; 30g brown sugar; 30g butter, melted; 1 teaspoon cinnamon

Instructions:
1. Place apple halves in a baking dish.
2. In a bowl, mix granola, brown sugar, melted butter, and cinnamon.
3. Spoon granola mixture into the center of each apple half.
4. Preheat air fryer toaster oven to 180°C.
5. Bake apples in the air fryer for 20 minutes until tender and topping is crispy.
6. Serve warm and enjoy these delicious baked apples with granola topping!

Nutritional Info (per serving): Calories: 180 | Fat: 8g | Carbs: 30g | Protein: 2g

Lava Cake

Prep: 10 mins | Cook: 10 mins | Serves: 4

Ingredients:
- US: 100g dark chocolate, chopped; 60g butter; 50g powdered sugar; 2 eggs; 30g allpurpose flour; 1/2 teaspoon vanilla extract; oil spray
- UK: 100g dark chocolate, chopped; 60g butter; 50g powdered sugar; 2 eggs; 30g allpurpose flour; 1/2 teaspoon vanilla extract; oil spray

Instructions:
1. In a microwave safe bowl, melt chocolate and butter together.
2. Stir in powdered sugar, eggs, flour, and vanilla extract until smooth.
3. Preheat air fryer toaster oven to 180°C.
4. Spray ramekins with oil spray and divide batter evenly among them.
5. Place ramekins in the air fryer basket.
6. Cook lava cakes in the air fryer for 810 minutes until edges are set but centers are still soft.
7. Carefully remove from air fryer and let cool for a few minutes.
8. Serve warm and enjoy the gooey goodness of these lava cakes!

Nutritional Info (per serving): Calories: 300 | Fat: 20g | Carbs: 25g | Protein: 5g

Fried Oreos

Prep: 10 mins | Cook: 8 mins | Serves: 4

Ingredients:
- US: 12 Oreo cookies; 120g pancake mix; 120ml milk; oil spray; powdered sugar for dusting
- UK: 12 Oreo cookies; 120g pancake mix; 120ml milk; oil spray; powdered sugar for dusting

Instructions:
1. In a bowl, mix pancake mix and milk until smooth.
2. Dip Oreos into the pancake batter, coating evenly.
3. Preheat air fryer toaster oven to 180°C.
4. Spray coated Oreos with oil spray and place in the air fryer basket.
5. Cook Oreos in the air fryer for 4 minutes, then flip and cook for another 4 minutes until golden brown.
6. Remove from air fryer and dust with powdered sugar before serving.
7. Enjoy these irresistible fried Oreos while they're still warm!

Nutritional Info (per serving): Calories: 250 | Fat: 10g | Carbs: 35g | Protein: 3g

Baked S'mores Cups
Prep: 15 mins | Cook: 10 mins | Serves: 6
Ingredients:
- US: 6 graham crackers; 120g chocolate chips; 120g mini marshmallows; oil spray
- UK: 6 graham crackers; 120g chocolate chips; 120g mini marshmallows; oil spray

Instructions:
1. Preheat air fryer toaster oven to 180°C.
2. Place graham crackers in the bottom of muffin cups.
3. Top each graham cracker with chocolate chips and mini marshmallows.
4. Spray the tops with oil spray.
5. Bake s'mores cups in the air fryer for 8-10 minutes until marshmallows are golden brown and chocolate is melted.
6. Remove from air fryer and let cool slightly before serving.
7. Enjoy these delicious baked s'mores cups as a sweet treat!

Nutritional Info (per serving): Calories: 200 | Fat: 8g | Carbs: 30g | Protein: 2g

Churro Bites
Prep: 15 mins | Cook: 10 mins | Serves: 4
Ingredients:
- US: 250ml water; 60g butter; 1 tablespoon granulated sugar; 1/4 teaspoon salt; 150g allpurpose flour; 1 egg; oil spray; 50g granulated sugar mixed with 1 teaspoon cinnamon
- UK: 250ml water; 60g butter; 1 tablespoon granulated sugar; 1/4 teaspoon salt; 150g allpurpose flour; 1 egg; oil spray; 50g granulated sugar mixed with 1 teaspoon cinnamon

Instructions:
1. In a saucepan, bring water, butter, sugar, and salt to a boil.
2. Remove from heat and stir in flour until a dough forms.
3. Let cool slightly, then mix in egg until smooth.
4. Transfer dough to a piping bag fitted with a star tip.
5. Pipe small pieces of dough onto a greased baking sheet.
6. Preheat air fryer toaster oven to 180°C.
7. Spray churro bites with oil spray and place in the air fryer basket.
8. Cook churro bites in the air fryer for 8-10 minutes until golden brown.
9. Roll warm churro bites in cinnamon sugar mixture until coated.
10. Enjoy these crispy and sweet churro bites as a delightful dessert!

Nutritional Info (per serving): Calories: 220 | Fat: 10g | Carbs: 30g | Protein: 3g

Pineapple Upside Down Cakes

Prep: 20 mins | Cook: 15 mins | Serves: 4

Ingredients:
- US: 1 can pineapple slices, drained; 4 maraschino cherries; 120g allpurpose flour; 100g granulated sugar; 1 teaspoon baking powder; 1/4 teaspoon salt; 60ml pineapple juice; 30ml vegetable oil; 1 egg
- UK: 1 can pineapple slices, drained; 4 maraschino cherries; 120g allpurpose flour; 100g granulated sugar; 1 teaspoon baking powder; 1/4 teaspoon salt; 60ml pineapple juice; 30ml vegetable oil; 1 egg

Instructions:
1. Place pineapple slices in the bottom of greased muffin cups.
2. Put a maraschino cherry in the center of each pineapple slice.
3. In a bowl, mix flour, sugar, baking powder, and salt.
4. Stir in pineapple juice, vegetable oil, and egg until smooth.
5. Pour batter over pineapple slices in muffin cups.
6. Preheat air fryer toaster oven to 180°C.
7. Bake pineapple upside down cakes in the air fryer for 1215 minutes until golden brown and cooked through.
8. Remove from air fryer and let cool slightly before serving.
9. Enjoy these adorable pineapple upside down cakes with a tropical twist!

Nutritional Info (per serving): Calories: 250 | Fat: 8g | Carbs: 40g | Protein: 3g

Red Velvet Lava Crunch Cake

Prep: 20 mins | Cook: 10 mins | Serves: 4

Ingredients:
- US: 100g dark chocolate, chopped; 60g butter; 50g powdered sugar; 2 eggs; 30g allpurpose flour; 1/2 teaspoon red food coloring; oil spray
- UK: 100g dark chocolate, chopped; 60g butter; 50g powdered sugar; 2 eggs; 30g allpurpose flour; 1/2 teaspoon red food coloring; oil spray

Instructions:
1. In a microwavesafe bowl, melt chocolate and butter together.
2. Stir in powdered sugar, eggs, flour, and red food coloring until smooth.
3. Preheat air fryer toaster oven to 180°C.
4. Spray ramekins with oil spray and divide batter evenly among them.
5. Place ramekins in the air fryer basket.
6. Cook lava cakes in the air fryer for 810 minutes until edges are set but centers are still soft.
7. Carefully remove from air fryer and let cool for a few minutes.
8. Serve warm and enjoy the rich, decadent goodness of red velvet lava crunch cake!

Nutritional Info (per serving): Calories: 300 | Fat: 20g | Carbs: 25g | Protein: 5g

Air Fryer Cookie Cups

Prep: 15 mins | Cook: 10 mins | Serves: 4

Ingredients:
- US: 200g cookie dough; 60g chocolate chips; oil spray; ice cream for serving (optional)
- UK: 200g cookie dough; 60g chocolate chips; oil spray; ice cream for serving (optional)

Instructions:
1. Divide cookie dough into 4 portions.
2. Press each portion into greased muffin cups to form cups.
3. Fill each cookie cup with chocolate chips.
4. Preheat air fryer toaster oven to 180°C.
5. Place cookie cups in the air fryer basket.
6. Cook cookie cups in the air fryer for 8-10 minutes until edges are golden brown.
7. Remove from air fryer and let cool slightly before serving.
8. Serve with a scoop of ice cream for an extra indulgent treat!
9. Enjoy these delightful air fryer cookie cups as a sweet ending to any meal.

Nutritional Info (per serving): Calories: 300 | Fat: 15g | Carbs: 40g | Protein: 3g

Strawberry Hand Pies

Prep: 20 mins | Cook: 15 mins | Serves: 4

Ingredients:
- US: 1 sheet readymade pie crust; 120g strawberries, diced; 30g granulated sugar; 1/2 teaspoon cornstarch; 1/2 teaspoon lemon juice; 1 egg, beaten; powdered sugar for dusting
- UK: 1 sheet readymade pie crust; 120g strawberries, diced; 30g granulated sugar; 1/2 teaspoon cornstarch; 1/2 teaspoon lemon juice; 1 egg, beaten; powdered sugar for dusting

Instructions:
1. In a bowl, mix diced strawberries, sugar, cornstarch, and lemon juice.
2. Roll out pie crust and cut into squares.
3. Spoon strawberry mixture onto each square.
4. Fold dough over filling and crimp edges with a fork to seal.
5. Preheat air fryer toaster oven to 180°C.
6. Brush hand pies with beaten egg.
7. Cook hand pies in the air fryer for 12-15 minutes until golden brown.
8. Dust with powdered sugar before serving.
9. Enjoy these delightful strawberry hand pies as a handheld dessert!

Nutritional Info (per serving): Calories: 250 | Fat: 10g | Carbs: 35g | Protein: 3g

CHAPTER 10: HOLIDAYS & PARTIES

Spinach Artichoke Dip Bites
Prep: 15 mins | Cook: 10 mins | Serves: 6
Ingredients:
- US: 200g frozen chopped spinach (thawed and drained), 200g canned artichoke hearts (drained and chopped), 120g cream cheese (softened), 60g shredded mozzarella cheese, 60g grated Parmesan cheese, 1 teaspoon garlic powder, salt, pepper, 1 sheet puff pastry (thawed)
- UK: 200g frozen chopped spinach (thawed and drained), 200g canned artichoke hearts (drained and chopped), 120g cream cheese (softened), 60g shredded mozzarella cheese, 60g grated Parmesan cheese, 1 teaspoon garlic powder, salt, pepper, 1 sheet puff pastry (thawed)

Instructions:
1. Preheat your air fryer toaster oven to 200°C (400°F).
2. In a bowl, mix together spinach, artichoke hearts, cream cheese, mozzarella cheese, Parmesan cheese, garlic powder, salt, and pepper.
3. Roll out the puff pastry sheet and cut it into squares.
4. Place a spoonful of the spinach artichoke mixture onto each pastry square.
5. Fold the pastry over the filling and seal the edges.
6. Place the filled pastry bites in the air fryer basket.
7. Air fry for about 10 minutes, until the pastry is golden brown and crispy.
8. Once done, serve the Spinach Artichoke Dip Bites hot as a delightful party appetizer.

Nutritional Info (per serving): Calories: 250 | Fat: 15g | Carbs: 20g | Protein: 8g

Air Fryer Jalapeño Poppers
Prep: 15 mins | Cook: 10 mins | Serves: 4
Ingredients:
- US: 8 large jalapeños, 120g cream cheese, 60g shredded cheddar cheese, 2 cloves garlic (minced), salt, pepper, 4 slices bacon (cooked and crumbled)
- UK: 8 large jalapeños, 120g cream cheese, 60g shredded cheddar cheese, 2 cloves garlic (minced), salt, pepper, 4 slices bacon (cooked and crumbled)

Instructions:
1. Preheat your air fryer toaster oven to 200°C (400°F).
2. Cut the jalapeños in half lengthwise and remove the seeds and membranes.
3. In a bowl, mix together cream cheese, shredded cheddar cheese, minced garlic, salt, and pepper.
4. Fill each jalapeño half with the cheese mixture.
5. Top each jalapeño half with crumbled bacon.
6. Place the filled jalapeño halves in the air fryer basket.

7. Air fry for about 10 minutes, until the jalapeños are tender and the cheese is melted and bubbly.
8. Once done, serve the Air Fryer Jalapeño Poppers hot as a spicy and cheesy appetizer.

Nutritional Info (per serving): Calories: 180 | Fat: 12g | Carbs: 6g | Protein: 8g

Pigs in a Blanket Wreath

Prep: 15 mins | Cook: 15 mins | Serves: 8

Ingredients:
- US: 2 sheets puff pastry (thawed), 16 cocktail sausages, 1 egg (beaten), sesame seeds, ketchup and mustard (for serving)
- UK: 2 sheets puff pastry (thawed), 16 cocktail sausages, 1 egg (beaten), sesame seeds, ketchup and mustard (for serving)

Instructions:
1. Preheat your air fryer toaster oven to 200°C (400°F).
2. Cut each puff pastry sheet into 8 strips.
3. Wrap each cocktail sausage with a puff pastry strip, leaving the ends exposed.
4. Arrange the wrapped sausages in a circle on a baking sheet, overlapping slightly to form a wreath shape.
5. Brush the pastry with beaten egg and sprinkle with sesame seeds.
6. Bake in the preheated oven for about 15 minutes, until the pastry is golden brown and the sausages are cooked through.
7. Once done, serve the Pigs in a Blanket Wreath hot with ketchup and mustard for dipping.

Nutritional Info (per serving): Calories: 220 | Fat: 15g | Carbs: 15g | Protein: 7g

Thanksgiving Turkey Fryer Sliders

Prep: 20 mins | Cook: 20 mins | Serves: 6

Ingredients:
- US: 500g ground turkey, 1 onion (finely chopped), 2 cloves garlic (minced), 1 teaspoon dried thyme, 1 teaspoon dried sage, salt, pepper, 6 slider buns, cranberry sauce, lettuce, sliced cheese
- UK: 500g ground turkey, 1 onion (finely chopped), 2 cloves garlic (minced), 1 teaspoon dried thyme, 1 teaspoon dried sage, salt, pepper, 6 slider buns, cranberry sauce, lettuce, sliced cheese

Instructions:
1. Preheat your air fryer toaster oven to 180°C (350°F).
2. In a bowl, mix together ground turkey, chopped onion, minced garlic, dried thyme, dried sage, salt, and pepper.
3. Form the turkey mixture into small patties.
4. Place the turkey patties in the air fryer basket.
5. Air fry for about 1520 minutes, flipping halfway through, until the patties are cooked through.

6. Once done, assemble the sliders by placing a turkey patty on each bun.
7. Top with cranberry sauce, lettuce, and sliced cheese.
8. Serve the Thanksgiving Turkey Fryer Sliders hot as a festive and delicious party dish.

Nutritional Info (per serving): Calories: 300 | Fat: 12g | Carbs: 25g | Protein: 20g

Twice Baked Potato Croquettes

Prep: 20 mins | Cook: 20 mins | Serves: 4

Ingredients:
- US: 4 large potatoes, 60g butter, 60ml milk, 60g shredded cheddar cheese, 2 tablespoons chopped chives, salt, pepper, 2 eggs (beaten), breadcrumbs
- UK: 4 large potatoes, 60g butter, 60ml milk, 60g shredded cheddar cheese, 2 tablespoons chopped chives, salt, pepper, 2 eggs (beaten), breadcrumbs

Instructions:
1. Preheat your air fryer toaster oven to 200°C (400°F).
2. Bake the potatoes until tender, about 4550 minutes.
3. Cut the baked potatoes in half and scoop out the flesh into a bowl.
4. Mash the potato flesh with butter, milk, shredded cheddar cheese, chopped chives, salt, and pepper until smooth.
5. Shape the mashed potato mixture into small croquettes.
6. Dip each croquette into beaten egg, then coat with breadcrumbs.
7. Place the coated croquettes in the air fryer basket.
8. Air fry for about 1520 minutes, until the croquettes are golden brown and crispy.
9. Once done, serve the Twice Baked Potato Croquettes hot as a delightful party snack or side dish.

Nutritional Info (per serving): Calories: 280 | Fat: 10g | Carbs: 40g | Protein: 10g

Cranberry Brie Bites

Prep: 15 mins | Cook: 10 mins | Serves: 6

Ingredients:
- US: 1 sheet puff pastry (thawed), 100g Brie cheese (cut into small cubes), cranberry sauce, fresh thyme leaves (for garnish)
- UK: 1 sheet puff pastry (thawed), 100g Brie cheese (cut into small cubes), cranberry sauce, fresh thyme leaves (for garnish)

Instructions:
1. Preheat your air fryer toaster oven to 200°C (400°F).
2. Roll out the puff pastry sheet and cut it into small squares.
3. Place a cube of Brie cheese on each pastry square.
4. Top the Brie with a small spoonful of cranberry sauce.
5. Fold the pastry over the filling and seal the edges.
6. Place the filled pastry bites in the air fryer basket.

7. Air fry for about 10 minutes, until the pastry is golden brown and the Brie is melted.
8. Once done, garnish the Cranberry Brie Bites with fresh thyme leaves before serving.

Nutritional Info (per serving): Calories: 180 | Fat: 12g | Carbs: 15g | Protein: 5g

Air Fryer Chicken Wings

Prep: 10 mins | Cook: 25 mins | Serves: 4
Ingredients:
- US: 1kg chicken wings, 30ml olive oil, 1 teaspoon garlic powder, 1 teaspoon paprika, salt, pepper, 120ml hot sauce, 60g butter (melted)
- UK: 1kg chicken wings, 30ml olive oil, 1 teaspoon garlic powder, 1 teaspoon paprika, salt, pepper, 120ml hot sauce, 60g butter (melted)

Instructions:
1. Preheat your air fryer toaster oven to 200°C (400°F).
2. In a bowl, toss the chicken wings with olive oil, garlic powder, paprika, salt, and pepper until well coated.
3. Place the seasoned chicken wings in the air fryer basket.
4. Air fry for about 25 minutes, flipping halfway through, until wings are crispy and cooked through.
5. In a separate bowl, mix together hot sauce and melted butter.
6. Toss the cooked wings in the hot sauce mixture until evenly coated.
7. Once done, serve the Air Fryer Chicken Wings hot with your favorite dipping sauce.

Nutritional Info (per serving): Calories: 350 | Fat: 25g | Carbs: 5g | Protein: 25g

Chili Cheese Nachos

Prep: 10 mins | Cook: 10 mins | Serves: 4
Ingredients:
- US: 200g tortilla chips, 200g shredded cheddar cheese, 1 can (400g) chili con carne, 2 spring onions (chopped), 1 tomato (diced), 1 jalapeño (sliced), sour cream (for serving)
- UK: 200g tortilla chips, 200g shredded cheddar cheese, 1 can (400g) chili con carne, 2 spring onions (chopped), 1 tomato (diced), 1 jalapeño (sliced), sour cream (for serving)

Instructions:
1. Preheat your air fryer toaster oven to 180°C (350°F).
2. Spread the tortilla chips in a single layer on a baking sheet.
3. Sprinkle shredded cheddar cheese evenly over the chips.
4. Spoon chili con carne over the cheese topped chips.
5. Sprinkle chopped spring onions, diced tomato, and sliced jalapeño over the chili.
6. Place the loaded nachos in the air fryer basket.
7. Air fry for about 10 minutes, until the cheese is melted and bubbly.
8. Once done, serve the Chili Cheese Nachos hot with sour cream on the side.

Nutritional Info (per serving): Calories: 400 | Fat: 25g | Carbs: 30g | Protein: 15g